BLOOD ON MY BRIEFCASE

BLOOD ON MY BRIEFCASE

30 Years in the Advertising Wars

Chris Miller

Copyright © 2004 by Chris Miller.

Library of Congress Number:		2004091927
ISBN:	Hardcover	1-4134-4954-9
	Softcover	1-4134-4953-0

All rights reserved. No part of this book may be reproduced or transmitted in any form or by any means, electronic or mechanical, including photocopying, recording, or by any information storage and retrieval system, without permission in writing from the copyright owner.

This book was printed in the United States of America.

To order additional copies of this book, contact:
Xlibris Corporation
1-888-795-4274
www.Xlibris.com
Orders@Xlibris.com
23715

CONTENTS

Acknowledgements 9
Preface 13
Chapter One: Saved by "The Wings of Man" 17
Chapter Two: The Biggest Martini in the World 30
Chapter Three: Fraternity Brothers with Expense Accounts 41
Chapter Four: Working Women of the World Unite! 52
Chapter Five: Lessons in Baseball and Expense Accounts 64
Chapter Six: Fire and Death in Houston 76
Chapter Seven: What Oil Company Conspiracies? 88
Chapter Eight: A Great "Spokesman" Who Doesn't Speak 101
Chapter Nine: Debbie Does Bartlesville 115
Chapter Ten: How to Become a Campbell Kid 129
Chapter Eleven: Firing Miss America 141
Chapter Twelve: Blood on My Briefcase 157
Chapter Thirteen: "Coke Is It" Meets "The Pepsi Challenge" 170
Chapter Fourteen: Wanda, the Wicked Media Queen 185
Chapter Fifteen: Who Says There's No Crying in Advertising? 193
Chapter Sixteen: Avoiding "The Hitler Channel" at All Costs 208
Epilogue 227

This book is dedicated to my family, which is responsible for any success I've had in my career, and all of whom have been very supportive of me in this effort:

To my parents, Doug and Nancy Miller, who think advertising is a bunch of people sitting around, trying to come up with catchy slogans and jingles.

To my wife, Karen, who thinks advertising is long trips, late dinners, and tough clients.

To my children, Doug, Andrew, and Sarah, who think advertising is getting clients lots of tickets to athletic events.

Thirty years back is a long time to remember things. And to protect both the innocent and the guilty, a few names have been changed here. But though others may recall some of them a little differently than I have, every campaign and incident in this book really happened.

ACKNOWLEDGEMENTS

*T*his book would not have been possible without the thousands of hard working, funny, and in many cases, eccentric advertising professionals I've met over the last three decades. These include co-workers, clients and media representatives. I'm grateful to all of them for making sure I never had a dull moment, even when we had subtle differences of opinion or were engaged in open warfare.

Several people have given me direct help in making this book possible. I am particularly grateful to the gentlemen who read and agreed to endorse the book: Herb Baum, Bob Bolte, Claude Caylor, Tom Latimer, John Oxendine, and Ira Tumpowsky. All of them were influential in my career, as well as encouraging to me as the publishing process took place.

I am also indebted to Bob Lansdowne, who filled in a lot of information about Tracy-Locke and its relationship with Frito-Lay. Lloyd Fabri did the same thing for me with McCann-Erickson and Coca-Cola. Susan McBrayer helped immensely with her honest comments and suggestions as the book was being written. And my mother-in-law, Shirley Kessler, helped by thoroughly proofreading the original manuscript for me, offering several useful suggestions.

A lot of credit is also due to my agent, David Johnson, who did a lot of soliciting on my behalf, providing professional encouragement and advice along the way. And speaking of encouragement, several of my personal friends read the early chapters and told me to keep going when I needed to hear it: Nan Cannon, Nina Fabri, Diana Reock, Ed Baker, Mike Kelly, Jack Morris and Rob Meagher.

Finally, my wife Karen deserves a special thanks for putting up with a few tirades while she worked her magic on the computer, printer and Internet as the book took form.

"People have the idea that all of us in advertising are oversexed, overpaid, drive BMW's, and will sell our souls for a great campaign. That is patently false. Not all of us drive BMW's."

—Young & Rubicam Account Supervisor, c. 1975

PREFACE

In 1970 the Vietnam War was raging, Richard Nixon was president, and the Beatles were still together. Box-office winners included *Love Story*, *M*A*S*H*, and *Patton*. The most popular show on television was *Rowan and Martin's Laugh-In*, followed by *Gunsmoke* and *Bonanza*. Radio was dominated by AM stations playing rock 'n' roll, with Simon & Garfunkel's "Bridge over Troubled Water" winning record of the year at the Grammys. *Life* had a weekly circulation of eight million, and *People* was just an idea. Another leading magazine, *Playboy*, was in a fight with upstart rival *Penthouse* over whose centerfold would expose more in each month's issue.

Advertising was rolling along as a $19.5 billion business, with most agencies privately owned by their founders or a very few shareholders. For the most part, they answered only to their clients and were filled with entrepreneurial spirit. Superstars such as Farrah Fawcett (Faberge) and Joe Namath (Brut) were being paid big money to endorse products. Gillette's Dry Look ("the wethead is dead") was being introduced, and Coke was "the real thing."

The year started normally enough, but by the time it ended some significant and lasting changes had taken place. The World Trade Center was completed, a Boeing 747 flew its first commercial flight, and Kent State exploded. Monday Night Football began its first year, with Dandy Don Meredith, Howard Cosell, and Keith Jackson in the broadcast booth. And at the end of that year, cigarette advertising was kicked off TV and radio, ending some sponsorships that had begun in broadcasting's infancy.

That year I was fresh out of college, beginning a career that would lead me into some of the biggest wars in the advertising game, including some that had raged for decades. There were the gasoline wars (remember Platformate?), the snack wars (remember "tastes as good as its crunch"?), the soup wars (remember "soup is good food"?), and the cola wars (remember "The Pepsi Challenge"?), among others.

Thirty years later, these wars, and lots of new ones, are still being fought. Some with different names, sometimes on different turf, but the battles continue. And the stakes are even higher now, with the recognition that established brand names are worth big bucks in these days of generics and product proliferation. As a liberal arts major, I knew little about how these wars were fought, but I knew I wanted to fight in them.

Five weeks after graduation from college I was in "boot camp" at one of Madison Avenue's biggest ad agencies, learning how to be a good "soldier." In this book I relate my experiences in these wars—how I went from knowing very little about marketing and advertising into an experienced "combat veteran." Along the way I met and worked with some of the smartest, most experienced people in the business. I also met some of the most bizarre, and in some cases, not-so-smart people in advertising. Whatever else they were, they were interesting people in an interesting business.

During those thirty years, I worked with some of the biggest and best companies in the world as clients. Companies such as Milton Bradley, Procter & Gamble, Gulf Oil, Frito-Lay, Pizza Inn, Coca-Cola, Campbell's Soup, and Texas Instruments. And even the smartest of them did dumb things sometimes. But even when they did, and took me along with them, I learned valuable lessons, sometimes about marketing and sometimes about people.

Along the way I had a lot of fun. Advertising, as they say, is a people business. The people that are successful in advertising have to genuinely like other people, and a sense of humor is a necessity if you're not going to get an ulcer or eventually be taken to the funny farm. But there's pressure, too. In advertising, you rarely do the same thing the same way twice. There's very little that's routine, and you constantly have to keep your wits about you, and watch your flanks and back. As someone once said, "In advertising, a friend is someone who'll stab you in the front." Advertising is war. But, as Napoleon said, "You have to be careful about war, or you may grow to love it."

This book is about the fun I had, the people I met, the companies I worked for, and the lessons about marketing—and life—that I learned.

CHAPTER ONE

Saved by "The Wings of Man"

Five weeks after I graduated from college in May of 1970 I had my own desk in a corner office in midtown Manhattan, overlooking Madison Avenue. So what if there were three other desks crammed in the office and three other guys sharing it with me? And so what if the four of us **combined** made less than thirty thousand dollars a year? We were in the advertising agency business, the industry that employed fewer people than Ford Motor, but affected every person in the country every day of the year.

We were working for Young & Rubicam, the biggest agency in the country, a powerhouse that billed $250 million a year in its New York office alone. All four of us were recent college graduates and had been selected over dozens of applicants to be in Y&R's Media Training Program. After three months of training we'd join Y&R's Media Department, and go on from there to glamorous careers in the advertising profession. That scenario was ironic, in that three weeks prior to that day, I didn't know there were such things as media departments. But I did know there were advertising agencies, and wanted to join one, and preferably work on an account that fought bitter wars with its competitors.

That would have to wait, however, as the task at hand was to make it through the training class and figure out how to get by on a salary of $6,500. Getting assigned into one of the five media groups that handled the media planning and buying for all of Y&R's clients was contingent upon completing the program successfully, then creating a special project and presenting it to a panel of tough judges from within the department.

That was the first step in Y&R's formula for developing media professionals. It had worked for decades, as Y&R grew into a leading agency, and as the dominant medium in America moved from radio to television. Since its inception in 1923, Y&R had been known as a creative-driven agency. Its campaigns for Jell-O, Excedrin, Sanka, Dash, Dr. Pepper, Cheetos, Tang, Gulf Oil, Lipton, Log Cabin, and Chiquita were known throughout America. Y&R's campaigns were responsible for the success of these and other leading brands. But unlike most other agencies, Y&R didn't consider its Media Department just a "back room" operation. As in other agencies the Media Department was responsible for recommending, then buying time or space in the right TV shows, magazines, radio programs, etc., making sure that those great ads reached each client's target audience. But Y&R's Media Department presented its own plans to clients, as opposed to many other agencies where the account executives carried the plans over to the client and presented them. The presumption in those agencies was that media people all wore green eyeshades and belonged out of sight in the back room. At Y&R the Media Department was front and center, on the firing line right along with the creatives and account executives.

Y&R's Media Department was also charged with looking for new and innovative ways to convey the great creative messages to each brand's best prospects. One stunning example of that innovation: Y&R's Media Department had been instrumental in getting the ABC network to go "on the air" in daytime in the sixties. Up until that time, only the CBS and NBC networks had daytime programming, with ABC signing on later for primetime. In an effort to obtain lower prices for its clients who bought a lot of daytime television, Y&R had lined up several advertisers, including General Foods and Bristol-Myers, to make long-term commitments to ABC for putting soap operas on in the afternoon. It had worked, with ABC developing some top-rated soaps such as *General Hospital*. That move enabled ABC to eventually lift itself from being called the "third network," and ultimately move ahead of the other two in the midseventies.

But that kind of achievement was a long way off for us young trainees. Our first day of work was in late June. I took an early train from Katonah, as I was living at my parents' home in Westchester County until I could find an apartment in the city. I arrived at Grand Central Terminal about 8:30 a.m., walked the three blocks to Y&R's office at 285 Madison, and got there in plenty of time for the start of business at 9:00.

I met the three other guys who were to be in the training class that began that day. We were scheduled to train together for three months. After that we'd be assigned to a media planning group as assistant media planners and begin working on specific brands. That meant we did everything except get coffee for anyone who gave us an assignment.

The other trainees, Tom, Charlie, and Robert, had all majored in marketing or advertising at their respective colleges. At first I thought I might be "behind" the others because I had been a political science major, but it soon became apparent that we'd all learn 99 percent of what we needed to know on the job. We had an orientation class, conducted by Joan Kerrigan, one of the top administrators in the Media Department. She welcomed us and laid out our schedules for the upcoming three months. She said we'd spend time in various sections of the Media Department— Audience Measurement, Research, Spot Broadcast, and Network TV. Cable TV was unheard of at the time, except in a few mountainous areas of the country that had trouble receiving a decent broadcast signal.

We'd also spend time with the top Y&R media leaders in the area of newspapers, TV, radio, outdoor, and magazines. In fact, our "guidance counselor" for the training period was the top magazine executive at Y&R, a fantastic fellow named Constantine Kazanas. As we later found out, Constantine was a former Greek Orthodox priest, a gourmet, and knew more about magazines than just about anybody in the business, including most publishers. Y&R was a major magazine advertiser, and many publishers came to Constantine to ask about policies and pricing that they were considering before they made those big decisions. He was a great cheerleader for us and helped instill the high morale that was almost universal at Y&R. The commonly used description of Y&R by beginners was, "It's a great place to work if your parents can afford to send you there." And we soon learned that to be true, with money coming much later down the road. The overall atmosphere at Y&R was very collegial. That's not to say there weren't departmental rivalries, turf wars, or office politics. There were, but the overall concern was for the good of Y&R and its clients.

In addition to training us, Joan and Constantine had their other duties to perform. A little after eleven o'clock they told us to take an early lunch break, and to be back by two. The four of us walked a couple of blocks down Madison Avenue to a restaurant, ordered drinks, and began to get to know each other. We unanimously agreed that the reputation for long lunch hours in the advertising business was deserved, based on our experience that first day. We later learned that lunch was unofficially from noon to two, unless there was a need to meet a deadline, in which case lunch was skipped.

Our second topic of discussion was our salary level. We all knew that trainees made $6,500 a year, while secretaries started at $7,500. We knew that we were underpaid, even compared to other entry-level jobs at other agencies, but we recognized that there were dozens of other people who hadn't been selected by Y&R who would gladly take our places if they could. We also knew that there was potential to make a lot more as we became more experienced and valuable. We finished our lunches and ambled back to 285 Madison, ready for our first afternoon in the agency business.

Over the next few years I learned that lunch in the advertising world was a very significant part of the day. Business was conducted, connections were made, and impressions formed over lunch. Most of the people in media departments can have a "free" lunch every day if they want to, compliments of media representatives who want to sell them ad space or time. Some media buyers make lunch a very big deal, as the media reps have big expense accounts and can afford to go anywhere. The result is that lots of young buyers, influential in deciding where advertising dollars are spent, become regulars at some of the finest restaurants in their respective cities.

Within three months after graduation from the training course, I had been to places such as the Palm, Lutece, the Four Seasons, "21," Pen and Pencil, among others. At the Palm, lobsters were five dollars a pound, with a typical lobster running four to five pounds. Add a couple of drinks, some creamed spinach, cottage fries, cheesecake, and without any trouble at all you were eating a $50 lunch while earning $125 a week. It was amazing! I can't remember who first told me this, but a common piece of advice for people moving to a strange city is to check out where the mafia and the advertising crowd eat, and you'll find the best restaurants in town.

While almost everyone went through the initial "feeding frenzy" at the best places, some dropped out and started going to lunch with media reps only once in a while. Walking the halls of Y&R during lunch at that time, you'd see people having a sandwich at their desk, often from Conrad's around the corner, where the lunch line went out the door. Every day there was a poker game going on in one office, and a bridge game going on in another.

Whatever you did during lunch, you weren't really expected to be in your office between noon and 2:00 p.m.; people wouldn't call during those hours, except in an emergency. There was generally only one secretary on duty to answer phones for the whole floor. All this took place before voice mail was even thought of.

The four of us in the training program bounced around the media department over the summer, got to know each other, and learned a lot. At different times it was fascinating, tedious, exciting, and confusing. One thing that surprised me was the amount of swearing that went on during the course of business. It had been my impression that there would be a few well-chosen words during times of stress or crisis, but four-letter functionals were sprinkled liberally in most conversations and meetings, with both men and women participating. It surprised me, but didn't shock me, as we used pretty much the same language in the fraternity house in college. It seemed a little strange at first, but when in Rome...

We met a lot of different people, some very cool and a few strange ones. One day we were taken down to one of the creative floors. While offices in the media department were very businesslike, the creatives—copywriters and art directors—had all kinds of weird stuff in theirs. One guy had a bathtub in the corner of his office. It didn't have running water, but was one of the old claw-foot kind, with the four legs sticking out of the bottom holding it up. The office belonged to one of the senior copywriters, who claimed he could only write good copy while he was in the bathtub. He was good, so Y&R got him a bathtub. We didn't ask if he used it while dressed or not.

Y&R had a philosophy of learning about ongoing developments in the media world, whether it was a new magazine, a new show, another way to buy radio, etc. Every Monday morning there would be a presentation given by a media representative or group, usually involving something new in the world of advertising. We were taught to learn about these developments, and at least consider them for possible use by clients. A highlight of the training program was when Gloria Steinem came to the media department to pitch her new magazine, *Ms.*

Unlike most other agencies, Y&R kept an open mind about new media forms and looked for ways to use them. That was why Ms. Steinem, and Pat Carbine, a veteran editor of *McCall's*, were in Y&R that morning. The conference room on the thirteenth floor could usually accommodate the twenty to thirty people who attended the average meeting of this type. But with Ms. Steinem's celebrity status and good looks it was overflowing that day, even though the conference table had been moved and the chairs had been set up "theater style." When I got there, they were all taken, so I sat on the windowsill, sharing it with one of my training class colleagues. He noticed that the window was open, but I didn't, and went to lean back against the glass that wasn't there. He grabbed me as I started to fall back, and out. It was the closest I've ever come to falling out a window in my life, and I've never trusted windows on upper stories again, open or closed.

The two women gave an excellent presentation of their new magazine, which remains to this day a leading publication in the area of women's rights and advancement. *Ms.* has since restructured itself legally to a nonprofit status, rather than directly compete against its for-profit sisters. There must have been almost one hundred people in that presentation, the best-attended one I ever saw at Y&R, and I presume it got equal attention at other agencies. No wonder it got off to such a hot start. And here's a little-known fact: the first issue of *Ms.* was distributed as an insert inside the highly influential *New York Magazine*.

I became acquainted with one other aspect of the magazine world: complimentary copies. Everyone in the media department was bombarded with free or "comp" copies from virtually any magazine they could conceivably recommend to a client. Magazines were very generous in their offerings of comp copies to media planners, and of course to the lobbies of every department within the agency. One of the few exceptions was *Playboy*, a very hot magazine at the time. The attitude of *Playboy's* management was that their magazine was in such demand by advertisers that they'd limit comp copies to planners who worked for clients likely to advertise in *Playboy*. This eliminated the folks who worked on female-oriented clients such as General Foods, Procter and Gamble, and Johnson & Johnson, much to their annoyance. I was okay there though, as my first assigned account was National Distillers, a natural for men's magazines. The young men in the department, after stealing our fathers' *Playboys* in our younger days, thought it was fantastic to receive our own copy for free every month.

Y&R had a fascinating history, including its campaigns and its personalities. John Young and Raymond Rubicam were the largest of those personalities, though both had retired several years earlier. Mr. Young had died a few years back, but Mr. Rubicam lived in Scottsdale, Arizona, and kept in touch with the industry by writing an occasional article and making appearances at Y&R functions. Many people's favorite story about the founders centered around two campaigns that they had created, both of which became advertising classics. One had been for Squibb toothpaste, and used the tagline, "The Priceless Ingredient," to promote its benefits. The other campaign was for Steinway pianos, which the great ad men had branded as "The Instrument of the Immortals." A few years after he retired to Scottsdale, and rather late in life, Raymond Rubicam's wife had a baby. Upon learning of the happy event, John Young sent him a telegram reading, "Glad the instrument of the immortals still has the priceless ingredient."

And speaking of retirees and alumni, Y&R had a method to help its former employees stay in touch with each other. It paid two people to publish a quarterly magazine called *The Link* that was sent free to any former employee who requested it. The content consisted simply of letters to *The Link* from former employees. And today, thirty years later, Y&R still publishes the magazine. The letters talk about what the writer is doing, mention other employees they've spent time with, and recall the "good old days" at Y&R. The letters always include the writers' addresses, so other alumni can get in touch with them and keep the Y&R bond going.

Another story that circulated around Y&R concerned Ed Ney, who would later become president of the agency and, ultimately, the U.S. ambassador to Canada. Ed and a few of his lieutenants were going uptown for an important meeting, and hailed a cab. As they drove up Madison Avenue, the cabbie spotted the big portfolio case they used to carry storyboards and asked, "You'se guys in advertising, huh?" "Yes, we are," responded Ed. "Lemme tell you'se something," the cabbie offered. "I got nothin' against you'se, but it's all just a scam. Nobody believes the stuff you put out, but more power to you for foolin' everybody." The ride continued in silence for a while, until Ed said to the driver, "Sir, can I ask you a question?" "Sure," he replied, "whaddya wanna know?"

"What kind of toothpaste do you use?" Ed asked him. The cabbie quickly responded, "Gleem." "Why Gleem?" Ed asked. Again, the answer came quickly, "Because I can't brush after every meal," answered the cabbie in a matter-of-fact tone. (For the reader too young to remember, one of the leading brands of toothpaste in the fifties and sixties was Procter & Gamble's Gleem, whose tagline was consistently pounded into everyone's heads: "Gleem. When you can't brush after every meal.")

As we were going through the training program over the summer, I found an apartment in Mt. Vernon, New York. It was a former luxury apartment, built in the 1930s. It hadn't been luxurious for a long time and was rapidly going downhill. It was, however, affordable to me at $165 a month for one bedroom, and was only an eight-block walk to the Mt. Vernon train station. Even though I was only bringing home $195 every two weeks, I took it and moved in on September 1. I had a TV, a sleeping bag, radio, some kitchen utensils, and a few blankets to hang over the windows as curtains. As my table I had one of those big cable spools that a fraternity brother and I had varnished for use in our old room. I didn't have much, but it was all mine, and I could come and go into my own apartment as I pleased, answering to nobody but myself.

My girlfriend lived in Boston, and we'd go to each other's place every other weekend, but during the week it was me, myself and I, which I liked. My nightly routine usually consisted of taking the train home from Grand Central, walking to my apartment, then going to the White Plains YMCA to swim or play basketball. Once every so often I'd meet up with a fraternity brother at a bar to watch Monday Night Football. One night a week I'd stop in at the supermarket and pick up some food items. I was on a limited budget, so I had to shop carefully. Hamburger Helper was a treat that could be made and eaten for several days, and those frozen Chinese dinners that you boiled in a bag were considered a gourmet meal.

As time progressed, I got to know several TV reps with big expense accounts. They'd take me to expensive restaurants for lunch, and there were many fancy media parties to attend at night, so I never felt that getting good food was a problem. If desperate, there were hundreds of places in the city that had happy hour, with two-for-one, or sometimes three-for-one drinks, along with extensive hot appetizer selections as part of the deal. Every once in a while a few of us would partake of these deals and get a nice dinner in New York at an economical price.

In late September the four of us completed the training program and were each assigned to one of the five Y&R media planning groups, with the title of assistant media planner. Our graduation present was a one-thousand-dollar raise, which put us on an equal footing with secretaries, which was only fitting, as we'd now be producers, rather than pupils.

I was assigned to Gary Pranzo's group. Gary was one of five "group supes" who each oversaw approximately fifty million dollars in billings. That was a huge amount at the time, but now that expenditure level might be equaled by one good-sized brand. Under Gary were three media supervisors, and under them were planners and assistant planners—our new title. After a long summer of training, the four of us felt like fresh troops, out of boot camp and ready for battle.

Joining me in Gary's group was Tom Mullen, an affable guy who lived in New Jersey. We were assigned to share an office on the fourteenth floor of Y&R's building. We "roomed" together for about a year and got to know each other well. He knew when my love life was going well, and I knew when his engagement to a nice Italian girl was working or hitting a rough spot. He was living at home until he got married, so had treated himself to a nice little Datsun 240Z with his steady new paycheck. We were like two guys in today's cubicles, with little privacy and few secrets. I didn't mind. I had an office that actually overlooked Madison Avenue, and I had only graduated three months ago.

Tom was assigned to be an assistant planner on Procter & Gamble's Dash and Spic & Span brands. I was assigned a smaller P&G brand, Salvo, along with Old Grand Dad bourbon from National Distillers. It was purely coincidental that I was put on a liquor brand, but having been a bartender previously did help somewhat. I had seen, at the retail level, the loyalty of people to their liquor brands. I knew a liquor brand was a personal and important thing, and convincing people to switch brands was not an easy task.

But as a new assistant planner I was not about to be asked for my opinion very often. Instead, my first assignment was to keep track of Old Grand Dad's media budget, which had to be allocated on a state-by-state basis, **to the penny.** At first I didn't really believe that we had to keep track that closely, but a few months later I sent the budget to the client's bookkeeper, who called me to "reconcile" a twenty-five-cent discrepancy in the budget. I had not been able to find that twenty-five-cent discrepancy by the deadline, and had "forced" the planned and actual budgets to match up. Francine, the National Distillers accountant, was nice, but insisted on finding the missing twenty-five cents—out of a magazine budget that was over four million dollars. After twenty minutes on the phone without success, I offered to bring her a quarter myself, out of my own pocket—their offices were only a few blocks away from ours—but that wasn't acceptable, of course. We finally found it, and I was off the hook. But it did teach me that clients' monies had to be watched and accounted for carefully and accurately, though I never saw it monitored that closely again in my career.

While we concentrated on our specific assignments, there were three hundred other people in the Media Department working on other clients, and we interacted with many of them as we went about our business. Big accounts had large numbers of people working on them, and we all went to meetings together, lunch together, happy hour together, etc. We associated with planners, supervisors, and group supervisors who worked on clients such as General Foods, Johnson & Johnson, Metropolitan Life, Chrysler, and other household names. Sometimes we got to participate in the advertising efforts of our other clients, either planned or inadvertently.

Eastern Airlines was an example of that at a very early stage in our careers. Every once in a while, usually a Friday, an account executive on Eastern would walk down the halls, yelling something like, "Anybody want to fly to Boston, Houston, or Chicago for free tonight?" It was a strange thing to hear, until it was explained to me. It resulted from a new newspaper ad just being finished, with Eastern planning to run it in the next day's edition, or perhaps the next Sunday edition. There was no way to fax the ad, fedex it, or send it by satellite transmission, and certainly no E-mail. You had to physically get the ad "plate" to the paper to print from, and that required it being carried there, since there was no way to mail it in time. So Eastern, and other clients on occasion, offered to pay the airfare for a volunteer to carry the ad to the newspaper. Leaving on a Friday, the volunteer could then spend the weekend in the destination city if desired, with no airfare to pay. It worked out well for lots of people who could make a quick decision to travel and didn't need a lot of luggage.

Y&R considered Eastern an important account for several reasons. Most importantly, it was a twenty-million-dollar account. Secondly, airline accounts are prestigious for agencies to have, even though they're known as tough to work on. In the early 1970s, sighs of relief about keeping the account at Y&R were still being heard from the agency review that had been called in the late '60s. For whatever reason, Eastern had grown unhappy with the advertising produced by Y&R. They told the agency there would be a review, and that it was highly unlikely that Y&R would be retained—they wanted new blood, new thinking, and a new campaign.

But Y&R management didn't want to lose the account and decided to pull out all stops to keep it. An overview of the airline industry and Eastern's status was given to six or seven creative teams—typically a copywriter and an art director. These teams were then sent to separate hotels in the city and told to stay in their rooms until they came out with the greatest airline advertising ever created. They could order food, drinks, and women if they wanted, but they had to create great campaigns before they emerged.

The campaign that was selected as the best that Y&R had to offer, and the one it placed its bet on, was "The Wings of Man" campaign. This positioned Eastern as the "second-largest airline in the free world," with very serious copy playing up that fact. And making the ads even more serious and authoritative was the voiceover, provided by none other than Orson Welles. For those unfamiliar with his voice, he sounded as full as James Earl Jones, who for several years announced, "This is CNN." "The Wings of Man" campaign wowed the Eastern marketing department, as well as its top management, and Y&R won the competition. "The Wings of Man" ran as Eastern's theme for many years, was incorporated into virtually all the company's communication components, and became an advertising campaign classic.

As I was learning about past Y&R campaigns, I was also meeting various characters who sold TV time to the Media Department. One was Richard McLaughlin, the top salesmen for the CBS O&O (owned and operated) station in New York, WCBS-TV. Richard was a great salesman, someone who could sell to the tough, experienced "media queens" who populated almost every agency, as well as young, inexperienced guys like us coming up through the ranks.

The story about Richard was that he was such a good salesman that WCBS would overbook the amount of time it had to sell. This was way before the computerized inventory tracking systems of today, which enable station managers to keep track of exactly how many spots on each program they've sold. At some point the station sales manager would realize that he'd sold more spots than the station had available, and they'd have to bump some advertisers from running, meaning those advertisers were owed "makegoods" by the station. The "makegoods" owed would mount up until the station would have to preempt a national show and put on its own movie locally. This meant the station had extra commercial spots available, which they gave to those advertisers who had been bumped earlier. These movies became known unofficially as "The Richard McLaughlin Makegood Theater." It was a phenomenon I've never seen since, as TV salespeople have been given shorter agency assignments, and inventory management systems became almost universal at TV and radio stations. Also, Richard was a legend among television sales representatives, and there were few of those who could match his salesmanship.

CHAPTER TWO

The Biggest Martini in the World

So how did I get lucky enough to land at Y&R so soon after college? Two years before I graduated from college in 1970 I knew what I wanted to do—get into the advertising business, and work at an agency in New York City. My desire continued, despite the warning from my dad that "advertising is a bunch of people sitting around, thinking up phrases such as, 'Winston tastes good, like a cigarette should.'" I'm not sure where his perception came from, possibly from the time we were introduced to Shirley Polykof, the copywriting genius who had created that famous tagline for Clairol, "Does she or doesn't she? Only her hairdresser knows for sure." In any case, I didn't really think my father had it right, even though I believed most of what he'd ever told me up to that point in my life.

My perception of advertising had been formed by some magazine articles I'd read, along with that classic description of the business written by Martin Mayer, "Madison Avenue, U.S.A." And one of the best classes I ever took in college was entitled Public Opinion and Propaganda, Those were the "classroom" influences that made me want to work in advertising. But the practical reason was the men I had met who were working in advertising. I worked at Waccabuc Country Club during the summers, along with a few of my fraternity brothers. We were waiters and bartenders, so we saw the members at some of their weakest moments, when they were relaxing, informal, and off guard. The men in advertising always seemed to be having the most fun, and many of them also had well-spoken, good-looking wives, which didn't hurt my perception of them either.

Waccabuc is located about fifty miles north of New York City, and many of its members commuted to the city to work, several of them in ad agencies, while others worked in broadcast or for magazines. Waccabuc is a family-oriented club that people joined not for prestige, but to be "left alone." Most of the members were highly successful in their fields and didn't need to join a club for status, as they already had it. Many of the members were household names at the time, or headed companies with household names. While some of the members were old fogies in our eyes, the ones in advertising were mostly fun—they drank a lot, kidded around with us, the hired help, and in general seemed to be having a better time than most of their peers.

But one summer—the summer of 1969—there was a member of Waccabuc who seemed to be having a better time than anyone in the advertising crowd. That year, George C. Scott, had just finished filming *Patton*, and had decided to take the summer off. His daily routine consisted of playing golf at nine o'clock, finishing around one, then spending the rest of the afternoon on Waccabuc's terrace, beginning with two tall vodka and tonics. Since he was already a famous Broadway actor, not to mention his great performance in *The Hustler* and as General Turgidson in *Dr. Strangelove*, Mr. Scott had no trouble attracting drinking buddies throughout the day. But few people could keep up with him, as he was a big man who could hold his liquor well.

Let me tell you how well. Late one Saturday afternoon he was drinking with one of the few members who could keep up with him. John Sternberg was another big man (picture General Schwartzkopf) who was connected to the ad business. Mr. Sternberg was good-natured, a West Pointer, and a very successful headhunter in the advertising and communications industries. They had played golf earlier and had spent the afternoon on Waccabuc's terrace. Two of my fraternity brothers and I were setting up tables for dinner that night when Mr. Scott called us over. "Guys," he said, "I want the **biggest** martini in the **world**."

He was always friendly to us, but when Mr. Scott asked for something, we always jumped. There was something about him that said, "You don't want to get me mad." And when *Patton* came out the following year, everyone who knew Mr. Scott agreed that he didn't have to act very hard to be Patton, with his high levels of both temper and charm. We said, "Yes, sir, Mr. Scott," and went into the taproom, where another fraternity brother was bartending. We told him of Mr. Scott's request, and fast-thinking Sean grabbed a brandy snifter and filled it with gin and an olive. We took it out to Mr. Scott, who thanked us profusely and drank the whole thing. Yes, he needed some help leaving, but he made it out the door.

As usual, Mr. Scott was picked up at the club's front porch by his wife, who at the time was Trish Van Devere. She was a beautiful woman, an actress who had appeared in several movies, though none with the stature of *Patton*. She always greeted him cheerfully, thanked us for calling her, and drove off with Mr. Scott in the passenger seat. Whether or not she ever admonished him for spending so much time on the club's terrace, we never knew.

Later that summer Mr. Scott's quick temper came to light early one evening. He and John Sternberg had spent a long afternoon on Waccabuc's terrace, and it was almost time to call for his ride home. Mr. Scott was walking by a table of two couples, both fairly new members of Waccabuc. One of the men asked him to join them, possibly to impress his friends, but definitely not knowing how long he'd been on the terrace. After a few minutes Mr. Scott signaled me and I brought him another drink.

As I was putting it down among the other drinks and several appetizers on the crowded table, there seemed to some tension among the members. Mr. Scott was asking the others, "Have you ever seen my magic trick?" They all said, "No," and since I never had either, I left, but stood close enough to see what would happen. Staying seated, Mr. Scott pushed his chair back from the table and grabbed the white tablecloth with both hands. "I can pull this tablecloth off this table so fast that nothing will spill," he proclaimed matter-of-factly. The two women suddenly looked scared, and the two men glanced at each other with that "what-have-we-done?" expression. Just as one of the men finished chuckling, "No need to, we believe you," Mr. Scott jerked the tablecloth and said,

"Shazam." He was a big, strong man, but not strong enough to make the trick work. Drinks, ashtrays, and appetizers went flying, mostly on the two couples. One of the women let out a little yelp, and three waiters, including me, rushed over to begin the cleanup.

There weren't a lot of people on the terrace at the time, and no real damage was done. As workers, we weren't privy to the club's inner workings between the members. We did hear, however, that the board of governors sent Mr. Scott a letter of reprimand, warning him not to repeat that kind of behavior.

Besides Mr. Sternberg, another member who could keep up with Mr. Scott was Warren Bahr, who was the media director at Young & Rubicam. I would later learn that Mr. Bahr had appeared on the cover of the first issue of *Media Decisions*, a leading publication in the business for many years. As waiters and bartenders we couldn't help but see who could handle how much, and Mr. Bahr was definitely on the "A" team. In fact, around that time, his doctor told him to cut back, and drink only white wine, long before white wine became the drink of choice it is today. One of the funniest lines I ever heard Mr. Bahr deliver was when one of his fellow members, another advertising executive, began razzing him in front of several people about his new restrictive habit. "How do you like drinking all that white wine?" he teased. Without missing a beat Mr. Bahr came back with, "Well, I'm having fewer hangovers now, but they're more spectacular."

The following June, in 1970, I graduated from Dickinson College with a bachelor of arts in political science. Dickinson's a good school, but it didn't offer a major in advertising or marketing. I realized I'd be at a disadvantage in looking for a job in advertising, but figured if I could just get in the door somewhere that I'd be able to learn what I needed to know fairly quickly. I had my old bartender's job lined up at Waccabuc for the summer, thinking I'd look for a job on Madison Avenue on Mondays, my day off. Despite all the members who already worked in advertising I thought it would be presumptuous of me to approach them about a job. Also, I wanted to get in the door on my own, rather than through "connections."

I spent several days looking in the paper and going to employment agencies, trying to land a job anywhere in the business, without much success. Most of the jobs in the paper were filled by the time I made contact, and the employment agencies weren't at all impressed with my new diploma. And despite the fact that I had a high draft number and was unlikely to be drafted into the military, there were several prospective agencies who didn't want to hire draft-eligible men. And I'm not making excuses. I literally walked up and down the streets of New York, interviewing anywhere I could, willing to take any job at any agency. Based on the books I'd read and the stories I'd heard, I thought everyone started in the mail room, and I was prepared to do so.

While I never threw myself at any members of Waccabuc, several of them asked what I was planning to do now that I'd graduated, and I didn't hesitate to tell them that I was looking for an advertising job. All of them were sympathetic, and several offered to help. One of the first was Frank Mayers, who was president of the Clairol division of Bristol-Myers. He invited me down to his office in the city, and I quickly accepted. Mr. Mayers had an office the size of a basketball court, and he greeted me warmly. We had a nice conversation, and he gave me lots of good advice about getting a job.

The thing he told me that I remember the best was this: Advertising could differentiate between parity products, and in many cases was the primary difference between them. As an example he used Excedrin, a Bristol-Myers product, running those famous "Excedrin headache number xxx" series at the time. He pointed out that Excedrin was aspirin, with the exact formula—by law—as Bayer, Anacin, and all other aspirins. Bristol relied on its advertising, from Young & Rubicam coincidentally, as the primary method of getting consumers to choose a parity product over its competitors.

While this sounds basic to many people today, remember that this was over thirty years ago, when the general public was not as marketing savvy as it is now, and it surprised me, while making a lot of sense. It also heightened my desire to get into the ad game.

It was the first of many marketing lessons I was to learn "on the job," even though I really didn't have one yet.

The next big lesson I learned came soon after that, once I had a job. That involved Sanka coffee, then using Robert Young as its spokesman, dressed like the doctor he had played on TV. Sanka is decaffeinated and costs more than most regular coffees. The irony here is that the coffee beans used for decafs are typically inferior, and cheaper, than those used for regular coffee. Amazing! Advertising helps get a premium price for a cheaper-to-make product. I was already beginning to see why companies spent all that money on advertising.

Mr. Mayers opened a few doors for me at some of Bristol's agencies, but I still didn't land a job. So I kept pouring drinks at Waccabuc and walking the streets of Manhattan. I was invited into BBD&O, a leading agency, by another member, E.E. (Tooey) Norris. Mr. Norris was one of the top two or three executives at BBD&O. Later on I was told that he would have probably become president if not for a minor heart attack he suffered, and I believe it. I had waited on Mr. Norris for many years and saw that he had the ability to make anybody he was talking to feel as if they were the most important person in the world. And he did it naturally. There were occasions where I'd be serving him, and possibly one of his clients or friends at the bar, and he'd make both of us—his guest and the person serving him—seem very important. When I got the right amount of vermouth ("run out to the parking lot and whisper 'vermouth'") in his martini, he treated me as if I had just won the Bartender of the Year award with that drink.

Ten years later I ran across Mr. Norris again at BBD&O. I was working for Campbell's Soup, with BBD&O as one of our top agencies—they had both the "Red & White" Soup and Chunky Soup brands. I visited BBD&O's offices frequently. On one of my first trips there I made it a point to see Mr. Norris, whose office was bigger than my living room, had a conference table for six, and two phones that had cords that could reach to both ends of the room. As always, he made me feel more important than I was. We talked about the Campbell's business, which he had headed up at one time, and he provided good insight into Campbell. He said that Campbell was a great company, but to continue being great it had to "abandon the idea that it owed the American public soup at twenty-five cents a can." (More on Campbell's, and how he was right, later.)

Mr. Norris set up some interviews with several people at BBD&O, which I thought went well. I was sending "thank you" letters to them when my real break came. There was a big dinner party at Waccabuc one Saturday night, and Mr. and Mrs. Bahr attended. Late in the evening Mr. Bahr was having a drink at the bar and asked me how my job search was going. I told him it was progressing, but nothing definite had materialized. He told me to come to his office "sometime soon."

The next Monday morning I took the train into the city and called Mr. Bahr at 9:01 from Grand Central Terminal. True to his word, he told me to come ahead. Y&R's offices at 285 Madison were only two blocks from Grand Central, so I was there in no time. His secretary immediately escorted me into his office, where we had a nice discussion.

He asked me some questions about my draft status, future goals, and willingness to work long and hard. I admitted I didn't really know what the Media Department did, but would learn. I knew for sure that starting in the Media Department was better than starting in the mail room, so I'd be ahead of the game no matter what. After a while he said something like, "Well, I don't know how intelligent you are, but I know you're a hard worker. I want you to meet some other people."

With that, his secretary led me around for the next few hours to meet some of the top people in Y&R's Media Department. I didn't realize it then, but these were some of the best, most respected people in any media department in the business. Among other things, I learned that Y&R's Media Department, led by Warren Bahr, had been instrumental in getting the ABC network to go "on the air" in daytime in the sixties. Mr. Bahr had also led Y&R's clients to sponsor TV broadcasts of Broadway plays. Clients seeking upscale audiences, such as Chrysler's Imperial, would pay a fee to the producers of *Company* for example, then buy time on a New York station to air the program, along with commercials for the pricey automobile. These programs attracted the affluent viewers that Chrysler wanted for the Imperial, but in far greater numbers than would watch on Public Broadcasting.

They asked me tough questions, such as, "Since you didn't major in marketing or advertising, how do you expect to compete with people who did?" ("I majored in political science, which studies what motivates people to vote a certain way; advertising concentrates on what makes people buy certain things—there seem to be some similarities.") Another one was, "Are you the kind of person who has a lot of **pretty** good friends, or a few **very** good friends?" And one asked, "What about you makes you different from other candidates we're looking at?"

I hadn't had too much experience being interviewed, but I thought they asked good questions, in that they made me think about answers on the spot, rather than having stock answers ready. Of course, I had been asked about not majoring in advertising during earlier interviews, so that one wasn't new. Later in my career I'd learn the common questions that most people asked in interviews—for example, "Where do you want to be in five years?"— and be ready for them, but these really made me think, and I walked out of Y&R feeling as if I'd revealed more about myself than ever before, while sober. Mr. Bahr told me he'd be in touch with me soon, but was noncommittal about a job. I thought things had gone well, but decided to keep looking. I also did some digging to find out more about what it was that media departments do.

Later that week Mr. Bahr's office called and asked me to return for another round of interviews for possible enrollment in Y&R's media training class. It was the first concrete ray of hope I'd had, and I couldn't wait. A few more days passed and I went back to 285 Madison. There I interviewed with more members of the Media Department, including Gary Pranzo, who was the top media person on Frito-Lay. I don't remember any of his questions, but he did offer me a sample of a new Frito-Lay product, Bugles, that was in test market at the time.

He also gave me some insight into test marketing: due to its headquarters being in Dallas, many of Frito-Lays' products, such as Fritos and Doritos, had a southwestern flavor. Before they were rolled out nationally, they were tested both in the southwest and other sections of the country to measure their acceptance and potential sales levels on a national basis. Remember, this was long before Mexican or Tex-Mex food gained its current popularity, and salsa surpassed ketchup as the leading condiment. Based on its performance in test markets, a product's potential sales can be projected nationally, taking into consideration the regional sales variations that may occur.

My interviews that day with Gary Pranzo and a few other people in the Media Department went well, I thought. They all seemed to be looking for the same qualities that most employers want: a desire to work for the company, the ability or potential ability to competently fill the open spot, and the right "body chemistry," as someone later described it to me.

"Body chemistry" was new to me as a concept in business— the desire of most people to work with people they liked, or at least feel comfortable with. I knew this was true in other types of organizations, as it had been in my fraternity, for example. But my naive impression had been that in business organizations the job went to the most qualified person. Throughout my career I've continually been reminded that being hired and promoted depends on "body chemistry" as much as ability, and that those in charge want to work with people they like and trust.

I must have done something right, as a few days later an executive from the department called and offered me a job. I would enter Y&R's media training class the following September. There would be three other people in the class, and we'd all be paid $6,500 a year. That worked out to $125 a week, less than Y&R was paying secretaries at the time, but then they were productive and, as trainees, we wouldn't be. I didn't care what they paid me. I was in the door, on Madison Avenue, and I had the whole summer in front of me to continue bartending, take a few trips to the Jersey Shore, and spend time with my girlfriend. It was the middle of

June, and I was ready to have the best summer of my life, with my dream job waiting right after Labor Day. That was on Wednesday.

On Friday I was still congratulating myself when I got another call. One of the people scheduled to go into the June training class had decided not to join Y&R, opening up a spot in the class of four. They wanted to know if I could report the next Monday morning. For about two seconds I thought about trying to find an excuse to keep my "greatest summer ever" plans intact. But I knew I had something special in my hands, and didn't want to take the chance that something might happen to it, and it wouldn't be good to decline an opportunity that dozens of other people had competed for. While naive, I did know that agencies were volatile places, where jobs came and went quickly. Those considerations, and the fact that I really wanted to get started, led me to say, "of course," very quickly.

That weekend, I made sure my one suit was cleaned and pressed. Other than that, I had nothing to prepare. I put in my last days at Waccabuc. My abrupt departure was not traumatic, as my coworkers knew I was trying to get to Madison Avenue, and they were happy that I had the chance, understanding that one had to strike while the iron was hot. I worked my shift on Saturday and Sunday, surprisingly without running into Mr. Bahr. In fact, even after I started at Y&R I rarely saw him, as he was so far up the ladder from me that I'd need a telescope to spot him.

I did keep up with him though, as he was one of the legends in the media business. As people would say about him, he enjoyed a long lunch, but was so brilliant that he could get more done in the morning than most people could do in two full days. His lunch routine was fairly well established. As head of a department that bought $250 million of advertising a year, every media rep in town wanted to take him to lunch, and Mr. Bahr complied. The only stipulation was that you'd always go to Antilade's, a great Italian restaurant on Fifty-third Street. Mr. Bahr had his own table there, reserved for him every day at noon.

That arrangement was a good one for almost everybody, but it occasionally led to some raucous scenes at the restaurant. When publishers or network TV vice presidents booked a lunch with Mr. Bahr, it was a great opportunity to bring along two or three of their colleagues to meet him and hear what he had to say. The lunches usually included several drinks for everyone, and lunch would sometimes run long. This didn't become a problem until six o'clock, when Mr. Bahr's lunchtime table was supposed to become Truman Capote's dinner table. There were instances when everyone was having such a great time that lunch ran past six, and Mr. Capote and his little group of friends would show up and demand to be seated. I'm sure you can imagine some of the comments and verbal exchanges that took place when four or five well-oiled advertising executives were asked to give up their table for someone in a strange hat using a cigarette holder.

Needless to say, I was never in any of those high-level lunch groups, but I heard about them, and knew it would be a long time before I could even hope to be there. And it didn't bother me when my fraternity brothers laughed at my meager salary. None of them were going to work on the world-famous Madison Avenue, in the glamorous and prestigious advertising industry. I knew I'd have more fun than they did, and if the ad game was cutthroat, insecure, and crazy, so be it. That's what I wanted. Little did I know that I'd have to work twice as hard as I had imagined, just to keep up.

CHAPTER THREE

Fraternity Brothers with Expense Accounts

In Gary's group there were three media supervisors, Mary, Eric, and Ira. Between them, they were responsible for planning on several accounts, including Procter and Gamble (Dash, Salvo and Spic & Span), American Home Products (Chef Boy-ar-Dee), National Distillers (Old Grand-Dad, Bellows), Milton Bradley (Playskool), Frito-Lay (Fritos, Funions) and some other household name advertisers.

The fifty million dollars that these accounts billed were equal to many large agencies at the time, both in New York and other cities. Our group was one of five media groups in the New York office, each with about fifty million dollars in billing. The $250 million that came out of New York represented about half of Y&R's worldwide billing at the time. Y&R was one of the three largest agencies in the country and world at the time. It enjoyed a prestigious client list that included some of the most sophisticated advertisers in the world: Procter & Gamble, General Foods, Chrysler, Goodyear, Metropolitan Life, Johnson & Johnson, and Frito-Lay.

Y&R had a long-term lease on the entire twenty-six-story building at 285 Madison Avenue, and occupied the entire building. Approximately 1,200 people worked there, with the media department located on the thirteenth and fourteenth floors. Through the single revolving door in the lobby walked some of the most accomplished and powerful people in the advertising world. Neither the main lobby nor the lobbies on each floor were flashy, but were described by some as "quietly elegant." The same could be said for the sixth floor, which is where the top executives officed, though it would be over two years before I was to set foot there.

Security in the building was lax by today's standards. In the mornings there was a distinguished gentleman in a suit who would direct people to the available elevators. He wasn't visibly armed, and wasn't around all the time during the day. The permanent "guard" consisted of two elderly gentlemen who ran the candy and cigarette counter right inside the door. One or both of them were always there, and the rumor was they owned the concession and made big bucks. There were receptionists in the lobbies of each floor, who presumably would challenge any outsider that got through the main lobby, but there were no sign in sheets, visitor badges or escorts. When I started there were no locks or secret combinations on the bathroom doors—those were added later. We didn't even have ID cards. Those were initiated about a year after I started, including photos of most people that were usually as flattering as those on our driver's licenses.

Women were careful about where they left their purses, and men kept their wallets with them, but overall, there was not great concern for one's personal safety or belongings. Overnight was another thing, however. Many people locked their office doors at night, but not everyone had a lock. Those who worked on P&G did, as the client required it. Everyone working on P&G also attended a "security" meeting twice a year, where they were admonished to abide by P&G's security rules: don't leave company documents of any kind unattended on your desk, don't talk about company plans in elevators or at cocktail parties, etc.

The agency treated everyone who came into it, whether client or junior salesperson, with respect and professionalism. In the media department, anyone who came in was greeted on the thirteenth floor by Dottie "Lobby." Her real name was Dottie Schneider, but she was so named because she maintained total control over the thirteenth-floor lobby, and had been there forever. She was known to media representatives from all over the country as the nicest, most professional receptionist in the business.

Dottie was single, lived with her mother, and made her career at Y&R the most important thing in her life. When a rep showed up to call on someone from the media department, Dottie would make sure she got his name right, and would immediately call the requested person and announce that "Mr. So-and-So" was here. As the rep waited, she'd ask if he wanted coffee or a soft drink and make sure he didn't wait too long. But the amazing thing about her was that the second time the rep would enter her lobby, Dottie would remember his name, even if he hadn't been there for a while. This was a big deal, similar to being greeted by name in an expensive restaurant, especially when a rep's new boss would come with him.

Dottie was also in charge of a payday ritual that she performed every other Wednesday, which was when Y&R paid everyone—twenty-six times a year, and those two months in which there were three paydays were great. Dottie ran a lottery every payday, collecting a quarter from anyone who wanted to play, and most of us did. At some point during the day, she'd draw a name from the hat in which all the participants' names had been placed, with the winner collecting all the proceeds. In my entire career, I never saw another receptionist who came close to Dottie "Lobby" in caring about her job, remembering that for many people, she created their first image of Y&R as they got off the elevator and walked into her domain.

Y&R was privately held by approximately three hundred shareholders. During our training period we were told that the goal to shoot for was to be a stockholder in the company, similar to making partner in a law firm. We might be considered for that honor, and the big money that came with it, after ten years at the company. But there wasn't any assurance that we'd become stockholders automatically. You had to be a key, top-performing employee for that to happen. Later on I learned that each stockholder was given a desk lamp that identified the person as a shareholder. This enabled stockholders who traveled to other Y&R offices, or met a new employee, to tell if someone was a fellow stockholder without having to ask.

I was assigned by Gary to assist Ira Tumpowsky on the National Distillers account. Most of my time was spent on Bellows, a low-priced brand that advertised, "Stock your entire bar for under fifty dollars." With Bellows, you could buy a bottle of gin, vodka, bourbon, scotch, and rye, all for about fifty dollars. It was their economy line, and received relatively little support, mostly in newspapers in cities where sales warranted.

Most of the ad dollars were spent on Old Grand-Dad, an upscale bourbon recognized as the "flagship of the fleet." The campaign ran in upscale magazines such as *The New Yorker, Time, U. S. News & World Report, and Travel & Leisure*. We also placed billboards in key markets, where there were high sales or good potential. We used all sorts of research to determine which magazines reached the older, upscale men who were Old Grand-Dad's target audience. The ads were designed to show them that they deserved the best in life, including bourbon.

One of Old Grand-Dad's major marketing problems centered on the fact that because its best customers were older, about 2 percent of them died each year. This concern was compounded by their younger replacements shying away from becoming bourbon drinkers. Instead, they were heading toward the "white goods"—gin, vodka, and even rum—as their drink of choice. This situation enabled me to attend many strategy meetings—I said attend, not participate in—where the age-old marketing dilemma was debated: should we target our advertising—both the message and the media spending—toward the older, current category users, or target younger prospects with the hope of converting them from noncategory users to category users, and ultimately our brand?

As so often happens in these decisions, it was decided to do a little of both. So in addition to keeping ads in the older-skewing publications, we began placing ads in some magazines that reached a younger audience. One of the magazines we decided to recommend was *Playboy*, which had been trying to get on Old Grand-Dad's schedule for years. Up until that time *Playboy* had been deemed too risque for the brand's image. But it was perfect for our effort to bring along new bourbon users and convert them to Old Grand-Dad. All the magazine research showed that its young male audience was affluent and tended to drink—heavily. The agency and the Old Grand-Dad brand managers wanted to add *Playboy* to the schedule, but upper management at National Distillers was still afraid it might not be appropriate. They finally gave in and approved *Playboy* for the schedule during the upcoming year. That's what caused the problem.

The problem was that *Playboy* was in a circulation battle with *Penthouse*, its smaller but fast-closing rival in the men's arena. Both magazines had shown all the skin there was to show, and were starting to show a little pubic hair in some of their Pet and Playmate-of-the-Month photos. In a race to be the sexiest, raciest magazine in the field, both magazines were showing more and more pubic hair in each issue.

As the war escalated, management at National Distillers became more and more agitated at what we were doing. Old Grand-Dad was in each issue, and as each month's advance issue of *Playboy* arrived, we'd anxiously open it to the Playmate pictorial and hope for the best. But the pubic war continued, and each successive issue showed more and more, though by today's standards it was tame. While we were convinced that *Playboy* was right for Old Grand-Dad, we dreaded the monthly ass-kicking we got from the brand management team. We knew they agreed with us and were just passing on the displeasure of their upper management, but it was time-consuming and frustrating in that we couldn't control the magazine's content. Our subsequent calls to complain to *Playboy* were greeted sympathetically by their sales representatives, but we all knew that the battle for circulation would not win over a few complaints by some advertisers.

We were all going through the motions, complaining about something we couldn't control, but unwilling to take the step to end the misery: cancel the schedule. This, of course, is a common scenario in the advertising world. A media vehicle, most often television, with a desirable audience starts pushing the morality envelope, forcing advertisers to choose between appearing in an undesirable—to them—environment or missing the opportunity to reach that desirable audience. In the end, National Distillers never ordered us to pull out of *Playboy*. Ultimately, *Penthouse* won the pubic war, and another magazine, *Hustler*, came out and made both the other two magazines look tame, so the issue went away.

Besides the fantastic lunches there were other perks to be had. Every once in a while our NBC representative, Alan Ewing, would walk down the hall asking if anyone could use tickets for *The Tonight Show* that night. It was unbelievable—here we were, having watched Johnny Carson while growing up, and now having the opportunity to see his show being taped "live." In those days, the show was taped in NBC's studios in Rockefeller Center, prior to its moving out to Burbank. All we had to do was leave the office a few minutes early to arrive at the studio before 5:30 p.m. when the taping began.

Alan was a great guy, a real gentleman who still wore a hat to work every day and had a great sense of humor. He called on us, representing the NBC-owned-and-operated TV stations around the country. His offers of tickets came whether or not we bought his stations for P&G or any other client. Alan knew we got a kick out of seeing *The Tonight Show*, and he'd been around long enough to know that we'd cut him a break when we could—even though we rookies didn't know that yet.

The first time he passed some tickets around, four of us from our training class got them and headed over to Rockefeller Center. We got there in time and saw the show from regular seats—no VIP section, no backstage visit with Ed McMahan or Johnny. In fact, the guest host that night was Tony Randall. My first reaction was to notice how small the set was. Johnny's (Tony's) desk was fairly close to the band on the right, led by Doc Severinson, and when Ed crooned, "Heeeeerrrrr's Johnny!" he was very close on the left. It was a kick to see the show being taped, then go home and watch it at 11:30 again. I guess we were easily amused, but it was fun. And we all thought how great it would be to bring our girlfriends one night. But it was always a last-minute thing, so it never happened to me, especially since my girlfriend at the time lived in Boston.

In addition to working on National Distillers, I was assigned to work on a P&G brand, Salvo. It was an interesting assignment in many ways, especially because it was one of the few P&G products that failed. That company tested and retested every product before introducing it nationally. In fact, most copy and/or media-spending tests for P&G brands were planned to last at least a year before they were reformulated, killed, or rolled out nationally.

Salvo had gone through that process and had been introduced nationally. It was a new concept for a detergent. It was designed to liberate the downtrodden "housewife" from having to measure and pour detergent into the washer. She simply unwrapped two Salvo tablets and dropped them into the washer along with the laundry, turned it on and walked away, with extra time to carry out her other household duties. In fact, Salvo was considered so efficient that the target audience was not "housewives" but "working women." Accordingly, the TV buying strategy called for the purchase of very little daytime television, almost heresy for the company that had practically invented the "soap opera," and instead used early evening and primetime, with special emphasis on a new show that was attracting large numbers of working women called *60 Minutes*. Leaving the soap operas behind required special approval from P&G's top management. The company still owned six soaps, including three like *As the World Turns* that Y&R produced for them. This was a holdover from the early days of broadcast when advertising agencies produced the programs that their clients sponsored.

Salvo began having problems soon after it came out of test market and went national. In some areas, where the water wasn't conducive to completely dissolving the tablets, horrified women unloaded their wash, only to find half-dissolved tablets stuck to their husbands' best shirts. And Salvo had high levels of phosphates in its formula. During the early '70s several large municipalities banned or reduced acceptable amounts of phosphates in soaps and detergents sold in their areas.

Add to these problems the fact that using detergent tablets was a new concept to women—in a heavily advertised category with relatively little product differentiation—and you had a brand fighting for its life. Salvo's media budget kept getting reduced each year, and the areas in which we placed local or spot TV support kept shrinking. Despite P&G's efforts at reformulation, and Y&R's advertising efforts—no agency wanted to be associated with an unsuccessful brand from the world's most sophisticated advertiser—Salvo was eventually pulled off the market. Those of us who worked on it thus became members of a small club within the advertising community: people who have worked on a failed product from P&G. To this day, there aren't that many of us around.

As part of our job on our P&G brands—Dash, Salvo, and Spic & Span—we negotiated the television schedules in each of the local markets designated to receive additional support. This came on top of the extensive national network TV that was running. While we planned the broad guidelines for using network television, the specific schedules were negotiated and bought by the Network Buying Group within the Media Department. In conducting these local buys we dealt with TV reps from companies such as Blair, Telerep, and HRP.

The reps who called on large agencies such as Y&R were typically the best in the business. They were usually smooth-talking, good-looking guys with young wives and a couple of kids, or perhaps a little older and divorced. In either case, they were veterans, knew how to sell, and were known at the best bars and restaurants in midtown Manhattan. They were older than we were, experienced veterans, and fun to be with while conducting business, eating lunch or having happy-hour drinks. They knew their business, and they knew their customers.

They knew how to charm the female TV buyers, young or old. And they knew how to work us young male buyers. They were like older fraternity brothers with expense accounts. One of the best reps, Brian Hogan from Blair, was a member of the New York Athletic Club. He'd take two or three of us there for lunch occasionally, but it wasn't just lunch. We'd go to the pool room, shoot some pool, and have lunch served to us at table side. We could keep playing as we ate, and there was even an attendant to rack the balls for us at the start of each game. I kept wondering, how much better could it get?

Another version of lunch was to go out with three Italian guys, who were reps from competing firms, but also good friends. When it came to business, they'd fight like hell for an order against each other, but after the battle they'd gather at a bar or restaurant for a good time together. They would also entertain us buyers in a group, and we would usually look for a way to spend lunchtime someplace other than a fancy restaurant. A common way to accomplish that with was to go to the peep shows in Times Square. Pat, Joe, and Pete would show up with bags of quarters—that's all it took to open the windows in those days—and we'd all walk cross town to the nudie joints. We'd have lunch "under the umbrella" at a Sabrett's hot dog cart on the way. The peep shows were fun, and we'd be back at our desks by two o'clock.

Over the next few years we learned a lot about media and how the advertising business worked. We also got somewhat spoiled as to where we ate and drank. With regard to living quarters, however, I wasn't spoiled. With housing being so expensive in New York, you had to look for deals, and be flexible. I kept my apartment in Mt. Vernon for two years, without improving it much, except for getting some curtains and dragging in a couch from the street. It made it easy to clean up after parties and overnight guests. To give you an idea of the place, the super was shot and killed within a year after I left.

In 1971 my old girlfriend's family decided to spend the summer in England, and asked if I would housesit for them. They had a four-story townhouse on West Twelfth Street in Greenwich Village, a beautiful place, and I quickly agreed. I'd live there for free and take care of the cat and the mail. Oscar the cat weighed about twenty-eight pounds, and was the biggest cat I'd ever seen. My other job was to keep the East Village heroin addicts from taking the TV and other valuables out of the house. Despite the fact that it had bars on all the windows, and three locks on each door, it was occasionally broken into. Having someone there would help discourage them, or at least slow them down.

I left a fraternity brother in charge of the apartment in Mt. Vernon and moved my few possessions into the townhouse. Getting to Y&R was a snap. I could get up at eight o'clock and catch the Eighth Avenue subway uptown at eight thirty, and be at work by nine. I had some great parties at that townhouse, some of them going on three floors at the same time. Amazingly, nothing was damaged or broken.

There was only one bad incident during my three-month stay there. About two o'clock one morning I was awakened by loud pounding on the front door of the first floor. It sounded as if someone was hitting it with a sledgehammer, which it turned out, they were. I slept on the fourth floor and looked out a window down to the street, where I saw two figures, one of them swinging an ax or a sledgehammer. I dialed "911" as fast as I could, and a cop car arrived within five minutes. The pounding had stopped and the figures disappeared. I opened the damaged door, and one policeman came in, asked me the usual questions, and looked around. The other policeman stood at the open door (this was shortly after two NYPD cops had been lured into an apartment, then shot by someone who didn't like lawmen) while his partner checked out the place. During this time, Oscar scooted out the door, never to return. It was the only bad part of the summer. The guys trying to break in got away, but they never came back. At the end of the summer I packed up my belongings and returned to the apartment in Mt. Vernon.

Soon after that summer my best friend from high school came back from Vietnam, left the army, and moved in. Dick Duffy and I had had the usual high school adventures together, and had remained in touch as Dick joined the army, went to OCS, then Vietnam, then back to Ft. Belvoir, then back to civilian life. He had a serious girlfriend in New Hampshire, whom he'd visit every other weekend, and who occasionally would come to New York at the same time my girlfriend was visiting from Boston. That made for some interesting living conditions on those weekends in our one-bedroom apartment.

Television commercials were highly restricted in the early '70s. This applied not only to their content, but even the **kind** of product that TV networks and local stations would accept. It may seem hard to believe in these days of "anything goes," but certain products—Preparation H and various laxatives, for example—were not welcome on television. Remember, at that time the programming content was also mild by today's standards. *All in the Family* was highly controversial, not only for its racial and ethnic humor, but also because viewers could often hear Archie flushing the upstairs toilet. The networks and stations felt it their duty to protect viewers from "unsavory" programming and products. It was about this time that Personal Products (a subsidiary of Johnson & Johnson) wanted to advertise Modess, a sanitary napkin, on television. Stations around the country were refusing to accept it.

Y&R had produced a very tasteful commercial for Modess, with a subtle reference to its use. Though it had received network approval, several local stations were refusing to run the spot, citing its content as not being suitable for their audiences. So the buying "clout" of Y&R's spot broadcast group was put into play. Stations who took the Modess ad could expect "most favored nation" treatment on other Y&R buys. Those that didn't could expect less business from other Y&R clients. This was a pure "power play," used by big agencies to help their clients break down creative walls like this one, or achieve other goals. The tactic was generally successful, as no station wanted to be left off the big schedules that agencies like Y&R purchased for their many clients. It was hardball, but as someone once said, "This is not a business for babies."

CHAPTER FOUR

Working Women of the World Unite!

After a while Tom and I started to feel as if we knew our way around Y&R and our assignments. We were still in a big learning mode, but we were contributing work for our clients, even though it was mostly crunching numbers and other forms of grunt work. All of our work was closely scrutinized by the media planners and supervisors to whom we reported. We interacted with them, as well as account executives, and people from the traffic, accounting, and forwarding departments.

Around this time, Y&R won the Milton Bradley account, consisting of Milton Bradley toys, headquartered in Boston, and its Playskool division, headquartered in Chicago. I was assigned to Playskool, which sold toys, puzzles, and games aimed at children under six years old. Obviously, five- and six-year-olds don't have much money, so the target audience for Playskool was their parents, primarily their mothers. We found places to reach them, including daytime TV and women's and parents' magazines. We looked for places to place the advertising that would provide an atmosphere of "caring" for kids. Magazines such as *Parents* and *Parenting* were perfect for this. And in the women's service magazines we found specific editorial opportunities that fit our needs. For example, in *Ladies' Home Journal* we contracted to buy space adjacent to the monthly article by Dr. Bruno Bettelheim, an acclaimed child psychologist. We also used a service from *Redbook* magazine that delivered samples, ad messages, and coupons in hospitals to mothers of newborns.

I occasionally helped one of my bosses, Eric, work on the Milton Bradley toy division, which used a lot of Saturday and Sunday cartoons to reach the older kids who could choose (and pay for) their own toys. Bradley placed a fairly senior marketing man, John Posten, inside Y&R to oversee our media purchases. He was given an office, and during the fall, as we negotiated and bought fourth-quarter kids TV programming, he "shadowed" Eric closely. We joked that they even went to the bathroom together. John was a veteran, a tough, but good client, charged with making sure that we bought the right programming. We had to satisfy Bradley's toy brokers in each market, a very important task in those days. This was before big changes occurred in the toy industry, with such things as the arrival of Toys "R" Us that diminished the importance of regional and local toy stores.

The three of us spent many a late night putting buys together that balanced TV rates with the desired programs in each market. Sometimes we'd work until nine or ten o'clock, then head to a bar for a few drinks. Depending on the hour we finished drinking, I'd either catch a train up to Mt. Vernon or Eric and I would take a cab to his house in Brooklyn with the meter down, a flat rate negotiated. Whatever the hour Eric's mother would get up and cook us some great Italian food while we had one more drink. Later in life, when I saw *Goodfellas* with Joe Pesci's mother cooking his friends a late-night meal after they had buried the body, I was reminded of these nights, but without the body.

We worked hard, and somehow made the deadlines and satisfied John and his colleagues at Bradley. Not only were we under pressure from the client, but the management supervisor on the account at Y&R was Peter Gorge. Peter was a demanding leader—which is what account service people were supposed to be—who was later to become president and CEO of Y&R. He was a brilliant strategist, good with clients, and once we gained his confidence, let us handle the media portion of the business while he directed his talents to other areas. While I can't say I predicted at the time that Peter would rise to such heights, I wasn't surprised when he did.

We weren't exactly writing position papers for the department, but we were asked to investigate and respond to various media questions that clients asked. One question I spent a lot of time on was asked by Playskool, the division of Milton Bradley that made toys for children under six years old. Obviously, these young kids didn't have any money, so their toys were bought by their parents, primarily their mothers.

The Playskool marketing people saw that women were continuing to enter the work force in large numbers, including women with children. The oldest of the baby boomers were starting to have children, and the percentage of mothers returning to work had begun to grow, and it would continue to grow dramatically over the next couple of decades. By 1973, according to the Labor Department, 49 percent of women with children were working. Playskool asked us this: with almost half of mothers working, is daytime television, with its mix of soap operas, game shows, and sitcom reruns, still an effective place to reach mothers with young children?

As the junior member on the Playskool media team, it fell on me to gather all the stats and prepare the preliminary response to that question. The answer would affect how Playskool would allocate its media budget for the upcoming year. It had traditionally felt confidant that a combination of daytime TV and women's magazines would effectively reach the brand's target audience of mothers with young children. Now, not only was the target audience changing its habits, but there were new magazines, such as *Ms.*, written specifically for working women, soon to be followed by others such as *Working Mother*. Of course, these new habits would also be considered in the new creative messages, but the creative team would handle that aspect. The Media Department gave them demographic data, through the account executives, to use as they formulated those messages.

What we found and reported was revealing, in that it quantified a trend that was becoming obvious. Right in front of us we saw more and more women coming into the advertising business.

Women were entering the work force in huge numbers, and staying there even after they had children. This phenomenon was a side effect of the baby boom generation that was moving through the population pipeline. I won't rehash all the well-known statistics about the seventy-six million of us born between 1946 and 1964. But it's important to note that as this bulge has moved along, advertising has catered to it, initially because of the money their parents spent on baby boomers, and then because of the money boomers now spend on themselves and their children.

A marketing axiom says, "You can't fight demographics," and Playskool wanted to be sure that their use of media matched up with demographic trends. More and more women were going to work, and remaining on the job after they had children. We showed these statistics to Playskool, along with our evaluation of how this impacted on women's consumption of media. Because these trends are so important to understanding advertising and media planning then and now, I'm including some of that information here. I'm also including data for 2000, so the reader can see how the trends we pointed out in the early seventies have continued today. I promise no more charts after this, but the one below explains a lot of things in our society today, as well as a lot of what's happening in the world of advertising.

First, the increasing percentage of all women (eighteen-plus years old) who are in the work force, followed by other facts pertaining to the increase in working mothers, according to the Bureau of Labor:

	1955	1973	2000
Percent of all women (18+) in the work force:	32%	42%	60%
Women as percent of total work force:	30%	35%	46%
Percent of women with any children who work:	28%	49%	73%
Women with children under 6 years old who work	16%	30%	66%
Women with children 6-11 years old who work	27%	46%	78%
Women with children 6-17 years old who work	35%	49%	79%

With almost 50 percent of mothers working in the early '70s, it would seem as if daytime TV might not be a good place to advertise toys for their young children. But further analysis showed that daytime TV ratings for mothers hadn't changed much over the years, despite more of them working. The reason for this was because many of them worked in jobs that weren't nine-to-five. Many worked at jobs such as waitressing and nursing, whereby they were still at home a good part of the day, and did watch TV during that time. Therefore, our recommendation to Playskool was that daytime TV was still an effective medium for reaching mothers with children under six, especially when combined with the magazines we were using, which also reached large numbers of working women.

Christmas approached, and even though the four of us were no longer trainees, there was one task that the most recent class traditionally performed at the Media Department party—we would be the bartenders. We'd man the two bars that would be set up on the fourteenth floor, where all three-hundred-or-so members of the department would gather. Each department at Y&R typically had its own Christmas party. Spouses were never invited, and members of other departments rarely attended. The atmosphere began heating up in the early afternoon, and we were summoned to set up the bars. There seemed to be every kind of liquor invented, with most being brands from National Distillers, and lots of rum. Y&R also had the Rums of Puerto Rico account, to which a lot of people always wanted to be assigned.

Right at five o'clock the department began partying. Obviously, I had never been to an "office party" before, but I was aware of how they earned their reputation as places where normal behavior was put aside as people drank heavily, many of them unaccustomed to doing so except on those occasions. That night I saw it all come to life. By about seven o'clock the party was in full swing. People were dancing, and a few had paired off and headed to empty offices down the hall. One senior member of the department grabbed a good-looking woman and dragged her into an empty office right off the makeshift "dance floor." She protested slightly, and a few semisober guys pulled the aggressor off her. No damage was done, and both the woman and male executive headed back to the dance floor—together.

A senior member of the Creative Department stopped in at our party. I'm not sure who invited him, but he may have been lost from the Creative Department's party downstairs. In any case, he had had a lot to drink, and at one point grabbed a wastebasket, took it into a corner, and relieved himself in it. Nobody seemed to care, the music got louder, and people began dancing closer and closer. I was putting the drinks down pretty quickly—"seven and seven" was my drink of choice—and feeling good.

At some point the four former trainees were released from our bartender duties, and we were free to roam around the party. I danced with several girls, had a few more drinks than I needed, and went down the elevators and walked to Grand Central to catch a train to Mt. Vernon. I managed to find the right train and track, and arrived at the Mt. Vernon station thirty-five minutes later, close to midnight. I began the eight-block walk to my humble apartment and quickly spotted something that I might have left alone had I been sober. It was a big couch, lying between the sidewalk and the street, right where someone had tossed it out. I stopped and examined it by the light of a street lamp, determining that it was in fairly good shape. My interest resulted from the fact that I didn't have a couch. I didn't have a bed, either, so my interest was further heightened when I realized it was a couch that also folded out to a bed. Despite its weight, and the late hour, I decided to drag the couch to my apartment, four or five blocks away. The liquor gave me extra strength, so I was able to muscle my new furniture piece down the sidewalk, through the outside gates of my apartment building, up a short flight of stairs, and into Apt. 1C. The next morning I woke up and determined that it had been a successful night on all fronts. I headed into the office, where everyone had an interesting story to tell about the party, but nobody had obtained a new couch and bed as part of the festivities.

Another account I worked on was *Fortune* magazine. A dapper account executive named John St. Leger ran the account at Y&R. It wasn't a large piece of business, but the agency also handled *Sports Illustrated* and *Time*, which both spent more and were marquee accounts. Working for Time Inc. looked good in new business presentations and kept the agency wired into developments at one of the premier publishing companies in the country. Our task was to promote each issue, both to prospective readers, by hyping the cover stories, and to the advertising/media community by touting the desirable demographics of their readers.

At that time *Fortune* was a monthly, with a much larger page size than most magazines, which are the size of *Time*. *Fortune* was known for lengthy, detailed articles, case histories of successful and faulty business endeavors. It had a tremendously upscale audience, but was considered by many to be textbooklike, not easy or fun to read. My job was to place ads in publications read by decision-makers each month as the new issue came out. We'd use magazines such as *New York, Advertising Age,* and *Advertising News of New York* (now *Adweek).*

On the day that *Fortune's* new issue hit the newsstands we'd run in the *New York Times*, and that's where the trick came in. *Fortune's* promotion director, Stanley Posthorn, always wanted to be on the back page of the *New York Times*—he wanted *Fortune* to stand out on the commuter trains coming into New York from all directions, as well as on the streets and subways of Manhattan. The problem was in those days the *Times* was printed in only two sections, and the back pages were in big demand by other media forms, liquors, and other upscale products. Everybody was fighting for those two positions, and I was designated as Y&R's procurer of that position, preferably the back of the second section for more visibility.

I was told by John St. Leger and my bosses in the media department to secure one of the back sections on the designated day at all costs. I could beg, threaten, cry, yell, or do whatever worked to get a back page in the *Times*. While we had the power of Y&R and all its media spending—"clout" later became the term—

the "Gray Lady" had power all her own and didn't feel very intimidated, though they did want a happy customer.

My contact at the *Times* was a seasoned ad salesman named Bob Czufin, who just retired a few years ago. He knew the score, knew that we were both crewmen on battleships that could blow each other up if they wanted to, and that we had to make something work. He often couldn't guarantee that we'd get a back-of-second-section page on the specific day we wanted, but was very good at offering compromises that would mollify, to a degree, the client and my bosses at Y&R. A solution might be that we'd accept a two-day window, with the guarantee of being on the back of the second section on one of those days. Another might be a guaranteed back-of-section position on the day we wanted, but with no assurance that it would be the desired second section. While Bob and I agreed, along with my bosses, that these compromises were acceptable, they didn't like it, and would let me know about it if the perfect position was not obtained on the designated day. Every month on that designated day I'd get up early, run to the newsstand for a copy of *The Times*, and find out how my day at Y&R was going to start. That little account, which took up a small amount of my time, taught me that it was possible—and necessary—to find compromises between powerful agencies and media giants when it came to buying media.

As I mentioned earlier, *Fortune* was not a big spender, but a valued brand for Y&R to have on its roster. At one point Stan Posthorn announced that it **would** become a big spender. Top management had decided to open the purse strings and spend big on a campaign to announce its move to a smaller-sized magazine with shorter, punchier articles. "There's no limit, this is a once-in-a-lifetime move, and we want the world to know about it" was the unofficial word passed on to us at Y&R. Several creative teams were assigned to come up with a breakthrough campaign. The creative teams went wild, coming up with important-sounding headlines, backed up by copy that made the new *Fortune* sound as important as the Rosetta stone.

In media, we began planning the usual print campaign, but

with spreads instead of the usual full-page ads. To the print we added radio in key advertising markets around the country, and threw in television in New York, Chicago, and Los Angeles. We made plans using different budgets, all much higher than *Fortune's* annual spending levels, ranging from several hundred thousand to a couple of million.

Egged on by everyone at *Fortune,* work continued frantically at Y&R to be ready for the big issue coming up. The next few weeks were almost frantic, with several extra creative and strategic planning people brought into the picture to make sure that big ideas and fresh thinking came into play. Excitement was running high on the day of the big meeting in the Time Inc. offices.

A troop of Y&R executives taxied uptown and assembled in a huge conference room. As long as it was, there wasn't enough room around the conference table for everyone to sit, so several of us underlings were arranged along the walls. Flip charts and storyboards were brought out and strategically placed on the table and around the room. A few executives from *Fortune* walked in and took their places at the table. I noticed some of the upper-level Y&R execs get puzzled looks on their faces. I later learned that several top Time Inc. managers who were expected at the meeting weren't there, a sign of possible trouble.

Ed Wetzel, Y&R's ranking exec, stood at one end of the conference table, got everyone's attention, thanked one and all for attending, and began the buildup for the presentation: "This is a big challenge, a great opportunity for us as partners, and we're going to show you some powerful advertising to serve an important magazine, etc., etc., etc."

Almost before he got started, *Fortune's* ranking exec rose and interrupted him. "Ed," he said, "we know you and your team have worked hard on this campaign, and that you're about to show us some breakthrough advertising. But before you start, we should, in all fairness, tell you that our management has switched gears and decided to cut back on our commitment to the launch of the new *Fortune.*" This pronouncement was met with the shock of dropped jaws, chair-twitching, and the nervous rubbing of various body parts by the Y&R contingent. Ed was the first to recover, and from the other end of the table fearfully asked, "How much are you budgeted to spend on the relaunch?" The response came quickly: "Fifty thousand dollars." This was greeted by more stunned silence, as the balloon not only deflated, but imploded. Nobody said anything for a minute as the shock set in. Just as the silence started to become embarrassing, one of the top creative smart-asses from Y&R stood up and asked, "Have you got it with you?" Amid some nervous laughter and some polite small talk, the meeting broke up. Needless to say, there was a lot of licking of wounds and drowning of sorrows that afternoon in various bars around 285 Madison.

We were inexperienced in many areas, and sometimes it really showed. One time a group of "young lions" was headed out for a fun lunch. There were six or seven of us, and we were celebrating one of the guys' getting engaged—to the daughter of a client, no less. On our way to the elevators the group passed Len Sheinfield's office, where he was intently working on something at his desk. "Come on, Len, we're celebrating," one of the guys called to him. "I can't," Len replied, hardly looking up. "Come on, what could be that important?" said another member of the group. "I'm writing a media plan for General Foods International Coffees, due tomorrow," Len said, putting down his pen, starting to consider joining us. Another from the group of party boys said, "International Coffees? Don't sweat it, that'll be a loser." Several of us joined him in declaring GF's new coffees to be doomed to fail, as nine out of ten new products suffer that fate. To his credit, Len declined to join us, electing to finish his assignment. There was a last chorus of chuckles from several of us as we again moved down the hall to the elevators. "International Coffees," someone said sarcastically, one last time. Despite the predictions of our group, General Foods International Coffees performed successfully in test market, was rolled out nationally, and became a huge, winning brand for GF. So much for our expertise in picking winners and losers. And to this day, the success rate of new products is still about one in ten, despite the highly sophisticated testing techniques that companies use.

One of the perks of working for an ad agency is that publishers give you magazines for free—complimentary copies—so that you'll read them, see how good they are, and then recommend that your clients place their ads in them. All of us in the media department received dozens of magazines every month, including four from the weeklies. The mail room used carts to haul all the copies to us as part of the daily mail deliveries. While fairly common now, the magazine industry was beginning to accept tiny samples from advertisers, and deliver them to their readers by inserting them in each issue. There were a few miscues, as when one of the women's service magazines accepted tiny, thin packets of liquid dishwasher detergent, attached to an ad page in each issue. The packets were strong and thin enough to be almost unnoticeable as one held an individual issue. But when hundreds of issues were stacked on top of each other for shipping, the tremendous weight of the magazines were too much for the foil pouches to withstand. They began bursting, with the liquid detergent leaking all over. The unlucky people in the advertising agencies got their sticky comp copies early, before a print production genius at the magazine figured out an alternative method for handling the printed copies without squeezing the detergent out of their packages.

Another insert came a few months later in everyone's copy of *Woman's Day* magazine. Each issue contained a Modess sanitary napkin within its pages, wrapped in plastic. All of us got our copies at the same time, and looked for the sample, having been told about this breakthrough delivery in advance. We all had some interesting comments to make as the magazines arrived. Some of the women were a little embarrassed about the product. Remember, this was the early '70s, and Y&R was involved in the fight with various TV stations to accept advertising for sanitary napkins. And we were all fascinated by the technology that enabled an advertiser to deliver a product—any product—in this manner. One other aspect of this event made it memorable for a lot of us. One of the planners in the department, Barney Silver, was known for being "thrifty," but his reputation for that trait increased tenfold that day. He went around to everyone in the department and asked us to give him our samples so his wife could use them. Granted, we weren't the highest-paid people on Madison Avenue, but most of us agreed that Barney gave "cheap" a new definition with that performance.

CHAPTER FIVE

Lessons in Baseball and Expense Accounts

These were the glory days of the television networks. There were only three of them—ABC, CBS, and NBC—and they captured 90 percent of the TV audience. The Fox Network hadn't even been conceived, and cable TV was something used by hicks in the West Virginia mountains to receive a signal. The Big Three were making money hand over fist, and weren't afraid to spend it on us in the advertising business. They entertained lavishly, and to be a network TV salesman—and almost all were men at the time—was prestigious, and meant you had virtually an unlimited expense account. No Broadway play was too expensive, no sporting event too exclusive, no restaurant too luxurious for them and their guests. Even lower-level media planners like us, with just a few years' experience, were treated like royalty. We went to Rangers games, Knicks games, Mets games, Jets games, Giants games and just about any other game we wanted to see, as long as it was broadcast on one of the networks. Higher-level executives went to just about anything they really wanted to see outside New York—the Super Bowl, World Series, Grammy Awards, the Oscars, you name it.

But the biggest event of the year for many took place in the city. Every May, in a well-orchestrated ritual, each network would introduce its new primetime shows for the upcoming TV season that would begin right after Labor Day. Once the new lineups were announced, agencies and their clients would huddle and try to determine the winners and losers for the fall season. This was an art for many reasons, the primary one being the fact that only about one of three new shows ever made it to a second season.

To help convince clients and media buyers that their new shows would be hits, each network threw a huge preview party, usually in a prestigious venue, such as a theater in Times Square. Lots of food and drink were followed by everyone—usually a few thousand—sitting down and watching clips from the new shows. Then the head of programming for the host network would get up and take us through their programs each night of the week and explain how they were going to get bigger audiences than their competitors. To help ensure that we got the message, stars from their new and current programs would be present, talking about their shows to the audience. When the presentation ended, the bars would reopen, the band would start up, and the party would continue late into the night. Normally tight-assed executives would be seen trying to do the latest dances in three-piece suits, with drink glasses in hand. Being late to work the next day was no big deal.

The most lavish preview party I went to was given by ABC in 1972. ABC was the number three network in those days. This was before Fred Silverman brought them to number one in the midseventies, with shows such as *Happy Days*, *Laverne and Shirley*, and *Charlie's Angels*. The number three network had to try harder, and always threw the most ostentatious, flamboyant preview party. That year ABC rented Lincoln Center for theirs. The main floor was ringed with bars and tables full of iced shrimp and hot meat, fish, and pasta. At either end of the floor was a stage for the bands they had hired for the evening. One band was Lionel Hampton's, and when they took a break, Count Basie's band came on from the other end of the room. Everyone agreed that this was a bigger deal than CBS' party the week before—they only had one band called Kennie Rodgers and the First Edition.

At about this time, I got a new boss, Pam Kroll. She was the first woman I had worked for since I mowed lawns as a teenager. Pam was promoted into Gary's group as a media supervisor, rewarded for her good work on several Y&R clients. She was known as a "tough broad," a taskmaster who worked hard herself and expected her subordinates to do the same. She was several years older than I was, single, and had kept herself in great shape. Besides working hard, she also liked to party at the right times. Before you get any ideas, no, we never became intimate, though we'd joke about it at times. Her closing comment on the possibility was always, "Forget it, Chris, I don't have time to teach."

I was warned by several people that Pam was a "bitch to work for," among other things. I decided to work hard for her, try to get along, and hope for the best. As it turned out we became and remained good friends until several years later when she died much too early of cancer.

Pam put me on Grocery Store Products, the food division of Clorox whose products included Cream of Rice and Hidden Valley Ranch dressing, among others. They were undergoing a process I was to see many times over the years. A solid but somewhat sleepy company, sometimes family owned, would be taken over by a sophisticated marketer. A fresh marketing team, including a marketing VP and experienced brand managers were sent in to improve efficiencies and increase volume and profits. That's exactly what was happening with Clorox and GSP. Marketing and media budgets were being increased, and more was being demanded of the agency. Y&R was responding by upgrading the personnel assigned to GSP, and I was glad to be a part of it and determined to earn the confidence I had been shown.

I had done some preliminary work on GSP right before Pam came to the group and had gotten off to a good start with the new marketing team at the client, as well as the new account service team at Y&R. I knew Pam was inheriting several challenges and problems on some of the other accounts she was taking over, and I had enough confidence to ask her for a heart-to-heart talk. I told her I was ready to handle the GSP account, with all its brands and growing sophistication, by myself, as the "lead dog" in media. She agreed, told me to take charge, check with her at strategic points, and inform her of any major problems as soon as they arose. It's the way I've liked to work ever since, both with superiors and subordinates. It usually works well, except for "control freaks" above you and "slackers" below.

Over the next several months the Grocery Store Products team wrestled with several interesting marketing and media problems. Cream of Rice, a hot cereal, was fighting the trends toward cold cereals (quicker and easier), breakfast bars (also quicker and easier), and alternatives that could be eaten on the go, such as muffins, bagels, and biscuits. Hidden Valley Ranch dressing was a regional brand, popular in several Western states, but unknown in the rest of the country. It was a packaged mix that called for buttermilk, along with mayonnaise, as main ingredients. But less than 10 percent of homes kept buttermilk on hand, so it wasn't easy to make spontaneously. Their BinB mushrooms were expensive and canned, at a time when other major food companies were introducing fresh-packed mushrooms. The company also came out with a new steak sauce, Prime Choice, that had to fight the powerful, long-time category leader, A-1. All of these marketing challenges had to be addressed with creative messages, packaging, and other marketing tools, including media.

The target audience for all GSP's products was women, eighteen to forty-nine, with some additional characteristics—have kids, higher incomes, like to cook, etc.—and we developed media plans at several different levels for each brand. And each national plan required test-market plans, duplicating the national plan in two to four test markets, prior to running nationwide to see if it produced the desired sales.

Between all the national and test-market plans, and inevitable revisions as account service and the brand managers provided more input, I was kept very busy. I worked late three to four nights a week, gladly collecting the $2.75 dinner money that Y&R gave out to people who worked until 7:00 p.m. or later. It was hard work, but I was working with top people, dedicated to their jobs, all pulling together for the same result: successful introduction and expansion of the GSP brands.

Most of the media plans included the use of network television, along with national women's magazines to reach the various brands' female target audience. In the early '70s, if women were the target audience, daytime TV was usually the first medium selected. If working women were desired, women's magazines would be added. Other TV dayparts, such as late night and primetime, would be added as affordable. While not necessarily terribly creative, these combinations were effective, because there were only three networks—with much bigger audiences than today—and relatively few magazines, almost all with larger circulations than they have today. Simply put, there were fewer media vehicles with larger audiences than today's wider menu of media availabilities.

The Y&R team was led by the management supervisor on the GSP business, Phil Weinseimer. He was an experienced account man, able to act as the hub of the wheel, pulling all the players together—creative, media, research—to benefit the client. Phil commuted two hours each way from central New Jersey, but was always on time in the morning and ready to have a drink with the team after work ended. He was the father of two young boys, whom he obviously enjoyed teaching and watching grow. I remember him telling me one night over a drink how cool it was to get home and be asked by one or both of them questions like, "What's the biggest bomber in the world?" or "Who would win a fight between Superman and Batman?" I wasn't thinking about having kids, or even getting married at the time, but I could see how great Phil thought it was, and put in the back of my mind that it might be a terrific thing to experience someday.

We definitely moved the GSP ball forward, though we made some mistakes. An account executive got a financial report from somewhere that Heublein, the parent company of A-1 Steak Sauce, was too cash-strapped and/or unconcerned to mount a big counterattack to GSP's steak sauce introduction, Prime Choice. But almost as soon as we began Prime Choice's test-market schedule, there was A-1, running big-time television spots and dropping cents-off coupons everywhere in the same markets. This was a common tactic for category leaders to do when they saw a competitor testing. The increased advertising and the coupons, along with retail price reductions and other activity, were designed to make the test market unreadable for the new competitor. The increased defensive activity would theoretically hold back sales of the challenger, and the new brand never knew if the counterattack would be repeated as it was rolled out nationally.

Prime Choice was positioned as a "milder tasting" steak sauce than A-1 or Lea & Perrins Worcestershire sauce. It was promoted as suitable for use by the entire family, rather than just adults with more "sophisticated" tastes. In addition to trying to fog up our test markets, Heublein introduced its own milder sauce, called Steak Supreme. This came as a surprise to all of us, as the (faulty) financial analysis showed the parent company to be in poor financial condition, seemingly unable to launch a new brand. Despite the surprise counterattack, we pressed ahead with the test, and eventually Prime Choice went national, though it never overtook A-1 as the category leader.

Hidden Valley Ranch dressing was more successful. Despite efforts by Good Seasons, Great Beginnings, and other established package mix brands to kill it, Hidden Valley's great taste—and, we like to think, the great advertising—enabled it to survive and thrive in a very crowded category. Eventually the brand eliminated the need to add mayonnaise and buttermilk, moved into bottles and squeeze-bottles, and remains a category leader to this day. I'm still proud to say that I wrote and executed the first national media plan for Hidden Valley.

There's one sad note to the story, however, that's not Y&R's fault. Clorox Foods had purchased Hidden Valley from an entrepreneur out West who invented the formula. In transferring ownership and building the brand, nobody trademarked the "ranch" name, so today there are several companies selling "ranch" or "ranch style" salad dressing in addition to Hidden Valley.

In early 1973 I was called into Joe Ostrow's office for the first and only time. Joe ran the media department on a day-to-day basis, with Warren Bahr serving as the guiding light. Warren interacted heavily with clients, Y&R top management and various media properties that constantly wanted him to speak at their sales meetings and seminars. Warren was, in today's parlance, the CEO of the department, with Joe acting as the COO. Joe was known as a tough administrator, and when you were called into his office you could be pretty sure it wasn't because he was going to give you a raise.

I was a little nervous, but I didn't think I had done anything wrong, except possibly sleeping in my office a few nights earlier when I'd missed the last train to Mt. Vernon. In thinking about it, I figured Gary Pranzo, my immediate boss, would probably discipline me if that was the issue, but you never knew. I was relieved when Joe told me that Y&R Chicago was looking for a media supervisor to work on International Harvester. I would have to compete with a few others for the spot, but if I got it, there would be a raise and promotion involved.

I felt great about being considered for the position. But a little wind came out of my sails when I subsequently found out that in addition to being judged a competent media planner, as one of the criteria for consideration, there was another: the selected winner would have to be single, with no house or family, and therefore inexpensive to move. The Chicago position was a good one, but not big enough to warrant a high-priced move.

I had some concerns about moving out of New York, and had some serious discussions with my girlfriend about moving further away. She was still working on her master's degree in Boston, which was a doable drive or fairly easy train ride. Chicago would involve the time and expense of planes. We went back and forth about what we'd do if I got the offer, but never had to make the decision. I became one of two finalists who Y&R flew out to Chicago for a final interview with Dick Matullo, the Chicago media director.

Dick and I are good friends today, but for several reasons he chose the other candidate. It may sound strange to say, but I'm glad he did, even though I was somewhat disappointed that I didn't win and get the promotion. Chicago was cold, and my girlfriend and I avoided having to make a hard decision, and as it turned out, I got a better opportunity about six months later. Dick's and my paths would cross again, and for reasons that will become clear later, things worked out for the best.

During this time there was a group of young planners at Y&R, all male and mostly unmarried, who would get together after work fcase: 30 Years In The Advertising Wars

THANK YOU FOR YOUR PURCHASE
e-mail ACASSIDY@COX.NET

PACKING SLIP:
Amazon Marketplace Item: Blood On My Bri
[Paperback] by Miller
Listing ID: 0119T812530
SKU:
Quantity: 1
Purchased on: 21-Jan-2005
Shipped by: acassidy@cox.net
Shipping address:
Ship to: Victoria Dowling
Address Line 1: 110 English Oak Court
Address Line 2:
City: Alpharetta
State/Province/Region: GA
Zip/Postal Code: 30005
Country: United States
Buyer Name: Victoria Dowling

on Fridays and head to a nearby saloon to get the weekend started on the right foot. The places we went varied, but were all within a few blocks of 285 Madison. Around the corner on Fortieth Street was O'Brien's, a good old neighborhood bar, where lots of Y&R people used to hang out. It seemed to be open all the time, and there were rumors of a few people with problems who'd stop in on their way to work in the morning for a couple of quick ones to get them through the morning. I never witnessed this personally, but through the years met a few folks who I knew would have done it if they could. You never knew who you'd meet there, and in fact, at various times out-of-work agency folks would work as bartenders there. I knew better than most how such a job could lead to employment with an agency.

Another place was on Forty-second Street, right across from Grand Central, called QD McGraw's. QD's was a relatively new place, open and light, definitely not a neighborhood place. The owners knew the value of having a gimmick to attract patrons—the doorman was a midget, dressed in green as a leprechaun, who was friendly, ready with a quip, and held the door open gallantly for everyone entering or exiting. The Guv'nor was another place, just down a block from Y&R on Madison, that was a favorite stop on the way to Grand Central. They had a free buffet for anyone drinking there that was the best around—sliced meat, spiced chicken, little sandwich breads, meatballs. Lots of folks would buy one drink there and have their dinner very inexpensively.

On those Friday nights when we headed out, all of us were looking for more than one drink. Some guys just went with the group for a few quick ones, while others were ready to stick around and see what might happen, or what bright idea someone might come up with for the rest of the evening. If I joined the Friday night group it meant I wasn't headed to Boston for the weekend to see my girlfriend, and that she wasn't coming to visit me. That meant I had the evening free, so I usually stuck around through the night.

Sometimes the guys who were making a night of it would get up a head of steam, then cruise over to some topless place in Times

Square. Or we'd go to some hot bar on Third Avenue, looking for girls. On rare occasions we might go to a Knicks or Rangers game. This was usually voted down, however, as we hadn't planned ahead and would have to actually buy our own tickets. This wasn't very popular, as we had become spoiled by all the free tickets we received from the TV and radio reps, and didn't want to spend our hard-earned money on something we could get for free the next week if we planned ahead. And none of us was getting rich on our Y&R salaries.

Often it would get late, a lot had been consumed, and the bars would start closing. Some of us had missed our trains, some were in no condition to ride the subways, and most hadn't enough money for a cab. So those of us left would walk or stagger to one of the guys' apartments where we'd spend the night. The next morning was not a pretty scene: five or six guys with no change of clothes, no toothbrush, and no mouthwash, waking up at various times with bad headaches, figuring out how to get home. It was a great time of life for us, with no family responsibilities, and almost total freedom to do whatever we wanted on the weekends. We all took our jobs seriously, and worked fifty to sixty hours during the workweek, but when that Friday five o'clock whistle blew we were ready for action. Because some of these guys are now successful, happily married men, I'll leave it to the reader's imagination as to some of the antics this group pulled.

Another social activity we had was the Y&R softball team, called the "Media Misfits." The team played in an advertising league in Central Park. It had been dormant for a while, but a few of us decided to start it up again. We signed up twelve or fifteen players, then challenged a TV rep firm, Blair, to a game one afternoon after work. Brian Hogan, one of their top salesmen who called on us, immediately accepted, and volunteered to bring the beer. We played them in a long, friendly game in the Sheep's Meadow. We got a great turnout, both players and spectators, and quickly drank all the beer Brian had brought. I forget who won, but a good time was had by all. We played until dark, then headed to a restaurant for a party. We went to September's, located on the corner of First

Avenue and Seventy-fifth Street. It was a terrific place, owned by the husband of one of the senior buyers at Y&R. Drinks and food were reasonably priced, they had an outside section, and we got good service because of our connection. It became **the** place to go after our games.

After our initial game with Blair, we decided to bring back the "Media Misfits," and re-enter the ad league. So we began a regular schedule, playing once or twice a week during the summer, and even practicing now and then. All the games were in Central Park. I usually pitched the first few innings for the "Misfits," until I gave up too many runs or my arm gave out. I used a windmill delivery that I had perfected in college, and was pretty fast. This worked great until the other team got their timing down and used the speed against me. Once that happened, we'd bring in a slower, more conventional pitcher, and their timing would again be off.

We did fairly well, and had a lot of fun. One memorable moment for me was a game against one of our clients, Bristol-Myers. They were a major power in the league, due to the fact that they had a star player. Monte Irvin, the great New York Giants outfielder, worked in their PR department, and played on their team. Monte had played outfield for the Giants with another young player named Willie Mays. He was a big man, still in good shape, and a great softball player. I was pitching, and we had a two run lead over Bristol. I was feeling pretty good, but three men got on base, and up came Monte Irvin. I hadn't faced him before, so I had a fleeting vision of striking him out with my speed. I checked the runners, then challenged him with my high, hard one. Mr. Irvin whipped his bat around and blasted that ball so far over the left field fence that our fielder didn't bother going after it. A dubious award had been added to my list of achievements: the great Monte Irvin hit a grand slam off of me. I still enjoy telling the story to anyone who remembers the old New York Giants.

It was about this time that Tom and I received a lesson in expense accounts. We had been working on a project with the local TV buying group, headed by Gary Beldon. Gary was a big man who sounded and looked like Jackie Gleason. He was a real pro, with a great sense of humor. Tom and I had both been on business trips and were filling out expense account reports when Gary walked in. When we told him what we were doing he immediately went into a diatribe about the insanity of expense accounts and their documentation. He told us how a few weeks ago he had taken a multicity trip for Y&R. It had involved several different clients, and the paperwork was extensive. The Accounting Department, never known for their flexibility, had sent it back twice, asking for more documentation for some of the items. Gary had wrestled with the problem the first time it was returned, and was extremely annoyed when it showed up the second time. After working on it again, he sent it back to Accounting with a note attached to the front page: "There's a new suit in here. See if you can find it."

Several months went by and I was approached by Gary Pranzo about the possibility of moving to Y&R Houston. One of my many old bosses, Ira Tumpowsky, had transferred to Y&R Houston a year earlier as media director. Now the office was expanding, and they needed a media supervisor on Gulf Oil, the office's anchor account. I would again be competing for the position. I felt I had performed well under Ira, but knew that he would pick the best person to fill the spot, with familiarity a secondary consideration.

I thought long and hard about leaving New York, the GSP team, my parents, and girlfriend, who told me she wouldn't leave the East Coast, to go West. Despite some reluctance I decided Houston would be a good move, and went all out to convince Ira to select me when he came to New York to interview candidates. He later told me that I just did "okay" in our interview, but he liked the plans and client correspondence I had given him to read. He selected me to come to Houston, and I was off, with a new title—media supervisor—and a new salary of fourteen thousand dollars a year. As an added bonus, apartments in Houston were a lot less expensive than New York and Texas had no income tax. I didn't know it at the time, but Texas was to become very significant to me on both a professional and personal basis. The first personal change was my girlfriend telling me we were through, since I was so determined to go to Houston. By that time I recognized that our relationship had deteriorated beyond repair, so my move became a clean break for us.

CHAPTER SIX

Fire and Death in Houston

There was a lot to do to get ready to leave the East Coast after twenty-five years of living there. One of the hardest was to say goodbye to my colleagues at Y&R, though I knew I'd be back to visit fairly regularly. If for no other reason, I'd be in touch with the media buyers in New York, as Y&R's TV buying was centralized there. Each office bought broadcast media in its own market, but all other markets—network TV and network radio included—were bought by the buying group in New York.

My replacement on GSP was Tom Mullen, one of the guys from our training class, who I'd shared an office with early on. Tom had become an accomplished media planner. While I like to think that Phil Weinseimer and the rest of the team was worried that nobody could do as good a job as I had done, I knew Tom would pick up the ball and run well with it. To help things along, I wrote a brand-by-brand media status report, listing current and ongoing tasks, test-market situations, and national roll-out situations. This was in addition to the usual "turnover" meeting, where information was transferred verbally, and sometimes lost or misunderstood. This method of transfer was unofficially adopted as SOP later on, which meant fewer "dropped balls" when people moved off accounts.

Y&R's Personnel Department—now, of course called Human Resources—was superb in helping me move. They told me I could either drive my car—a '71 Mustang—to Houston and receive reimbursement at ten cents a mile, or just tell them I was going to drive it, and receive the same amount. I had about twelve months left on my apartment lease in Yonkers. I had moved there a year before from my first apartment in Mt. Vernon, and was worried that the heavy-handed landlords would force me to pay them the remaining amount due. Personnel told me to just move out and let them come after me in Texas. They'd have no real case, they said, if they re-rented the apartment with no loss in rent. Y&R did reimburse me for my security deposit, which I would definitely lose for moving out early.

Finally, they paid for the movers to come in and pack my stuff up, including garbage since they came a day early, and for transporting everything to my new apartment in Houston. I found that apartment on a weekend trip, where I felt like a kid in a candy store. Every apartment complex was nicer than the last. They were less expensive than the apartment I had in Yonkers, and the rent included use of their pools, utilities, and parking. And as opposed to New York apartments, where the super showed you an available unit, then adopted a take-it-or-leave-it attitude, the Houston complexes drove you around in a golf cart. There was usually a nice-looking lady at the wheel who put the soft-sell on you to rent a place there.

The movers came into my Yonkers apartment a day earlier than scheduled. I had prepared most of the stuff I wanted moved. They packed up everything including the garbage. They left some clothes and my cat, Hannibal. For the last month in New York I moved in with a fraternity brother who had a small garden apartment in Eastchester. I disposed of my fire-engine red '71 Mustang—with no air-conditioning—just a few days before my departure date, and stayed at my parents' house the last night.

Early on a Saturday morning in July I said goodbye to my parents, loaded three suitcases and Hannibal onto the train, and headed for the city. A bus ride to LaGuardia followed, and I checked in at the Eastern Airlines ticket counter. This would probably never happen today but because the ticket agent noticed Hannibal's travel box he told me I could bring him onto the plane with me if I didn't mind sitting in the back of an uncrowded flight. It sounded good to me, so I didn't even have to drug Hannibal for the flight.

He sat in his box next to me on the flight to Houston's new Intercontinental Airport.

We arrived in late afternoon and took a rental car to my new apartment on Westheimer Road, a few miles from the Galleria. My stuff from Yonkers had arrived and was waiting to be unpacked. I called Ira Tumpowsky, my new boss, and told him I'd arrived in one piece and would see him in the Y&R offices bright and early on Monday morning. As I was to quickly learn, the city of Houston ran on oil, so it was totally appropriate that I went to see a movie called *Oklahoma Crude*, starring George C. Scott.

The next day, Sunday, was clear and hot, with an afternoon thundershower that is typical for Houston. The daily question is, how much will it rain, and will areas of the city flood, making for interesting afternoon commutes? Houston weather turned out to be the most extreme of any city I've ever lived in. I like hot weather, so it didn't bother me much, but most people find it stifling. As they say, it was "the humidity." In fact, at going-away parties, both office and private, the custom was to give gag-gifts, with the last one being a bottle of Houston air: a bottle filled with a mixture of one-half water and one-half air.

During my time in Houston several hurricanes blew up the Texas coastline and hit the city pretty hard. Y&R's office was on the fifth floor of the United Gas building downtown. It had about forty stories, and was made to sway in high winds. A few times I saw people coming down from the upper floors, some claiming to be afraid, others claiming to be seasick.

At one point a major hurricane came up the coast and brought so much rain that the entire city was flooded. We left work to avoid the inevitable traffic jam, but couldn't even get to the parking lot because of the two feet of water on the sidewalks. So we adjourned to the bar in the bottom of the building and waited for the water and traffic to diminish. The good thing about Houston was that even though it flooded with a good rain, it drained well, and the floods didn't last long. That night, however, it didn't help one fellow, an out-of-towner staying at the Shamrock Hilton hotel.

The Shamrock was the hotel where they held the big party in the movie *Giant*, and it had the biggest swimming pool I'd ever seen. Before I saw it, someone told me they had water skiing pageants in it, and I didn't believe it. But when I saw it I realized it was so big that it definitely could handle a ski boat and skiers. It was in back of the Shamrock and seemed to take up an entire city block. During the hurricane a poor traveler that night was driving his rental car back to the hotel. The water was above his hubcaps, and he became disoriented. Thinking the wide open space ahead was a parking lot, he drove right into the pool. Luckily, the car sank slowly enough so that he was able to get out safely.

On Monday morning I was in the office by 8:00 a.m., which was the official time Y&R opened. Of course, being in the central time zone meant it was 9:00 a.m. in New York. Houston was an early city, as employees of the major oil companies started at 7:00 or 7:30 a.m. and left at 3:30 or 4:00 p.m. I met with Ira, and he introduced me to the rest of the office, which was fairly easy since there were only twenty of us. It was a big change from the 1,200 people at Y&R New York, but I grew to like it. You could see the entire advertising process unfold, compared to the compartmentalization that existed in New York, where all the departments occupied their own floors. In the Houston microcosm, I actually saw copywriters writing, art directors drawing, print production people producing camera-ready artwork, and the account executives sweating as everyone prepared their work.

Y&R management had responded to Gulf Oil's request that it upgrade the Houston branch from a service office to a full-service office. Gulf was spending around twenty million dollars annually on advertising, a significant sum, so its "request" was as good as a demand. So from just having a few account executives to interact with Gulf's Advertising Department and relay their needs to New York, Y&R put a "mini-agency" in Houston, including creative, production, and media people who would interact more closely with Gulf, and become a self-sufficient, full-service office. And as long as there was an office there, it was free to solicit other accounts, if they weren't in conflict with other Y&R clients around the country. This was somewhat limiting, due to Y&R's size and long client list.

And speaking of Gulf as a client, they were tough, but fair. A lot of people think the oil industry is one in which the major companies collude with each other on prices, territories, and certain marketing activities. But they are very competitive when it comes to selling gasoline to the consumer. Any doubts I had about their competitive spirit disappeared one morning, soon after I arrived in Houston. Gulf had sponsored traffic reports on radio station KULF for several years. Those reports were delivered live by a traffic reporter flying in a small plane known as the *KULFBIRD*. While there was not a "natural," or meaningful match between "Gulf" and "KULF," the station was highly rated, and Houston's traffic had already become notorious. In fact, Metro Traffic, today a nationwide network of local traffic reports, got its start in Houston.

One weekday morning shortly after I arrived, there was a huge fire in one of the many oil storage tanks that ring Houston. Smoke and flames could be seen for miles, and the *KULFBIRD* left its normal flight pattern above the major highways to take a closer look. Unfortunately, it took too close a look, got caught in an updraft from the fire and crashed. Tragically, both the pilot and the traffic reporter were killed. Our sales representative from KULF called us that morning to let us know what happened and advised us that it would be a while before the station would be able to replace the lost plane and personnel. Upon hanging up I called the appropriate person at Gulf and advised him that the *KULFBIRD* had crashed, resulting in the loss of traffic reports—and Gulf's commercials—that day and for weeks to come. To my amazement, the response was, "We'll get makegoods, right?" Right then I knew there was a high level of competitiveness in the oil industry.

From this mini-agency we farmed out typesetting—no office had computers then—and TV and radio production was conducted in outside studios. But on our one floor you could follow a print ad from concept to writing and illustration, to production of the printing material, to final shipping to the specified publications. This sounds simple, but when you throw in getting the ad through different layers of approval at both Y&R and the client, it took a lot of time. "Everyone's a copywriter" is a favorite expression of real copywriters as they watch account executives and clients edit their work. Whether it's nitpicking or improving is in the eye of the beholder.

Most of us at Y&R Houston had moved there from the New York office, but there were a few "locals" on the staff, true Texans. As opposed to me, who hadn't worked on the Gulf Oil account, most of the New Yorkers had moved to Houston while working on Gulf. They had earned credibility with the Gulf marketing people, and a good, long-term relationship had been established. As always, it would be up to me to earn my spurs with the account teams, Gulf and the other clients.

The general manager of the office was an experienced, battle-hardened account man, Gene Hart. Gene was a no-nonsense kind of guy, with a somewhat sarcastic sense of humor. He was quick to get to the core issue of a marketing or advertising problem. He served as the top account man on the Gulf account, leading the strategic advertising efforts on that business, and led the office's new business efforts. Gene was a good delegator, expected excellent work from his subordinates, and was stingy in handing out praise. That was OK, because if someone screwed up, he'd let you know about it. If he said nothing, you knew he was pleased.

The most interesting person in the office was Ken Ventura, the creative director. Ken had worked at Y&R New York and Y&R Chicago, where he had been a co-manager of the office. He was an extremely talented writer. Several times I was in a meeting with Ken and Gulf marketing people, when they needed some print ads to respond to a specific anti-oil charge, with a very short time until the ad deadline arrived. The agency would have to get client approval, produce the ad, then ship it for overnight delivery at various print outlets around the country, all in less than a day. Remember, this was before satellite transmission of material—print or tape—was widely available.

On these occasions, Ken would take his notes, retreat into his office with the door closed, and begin typing on an old-style typewriter that he used forever. The entire office knew the heat was on and would wait for him to emerge. It reminded me of electing a pope, but without the smoke from the burned ballots. Within an hour, Ken would come out holding one or two pieces of paper containing his copy. One of the account guys would grab it and read it over the phone—this was also before fax machines—to someone at Gulf for approval. Very few changes were ever made to Ken's copy, and once approved, it would be produced and shipped to make the deadlines. Ken's long background on several major accounts also enabled him to think and write strategically when the situation demanded it.

Ken had a quick, wry sense of humor, and nothing much flustered him. The only time I saw him truly irritated was when someone questioned him about how much he'd spent on gas for a company car he had. He pulled the ten dollars in question and sent it back to the accounting people, with a note saying, "You probably need this more than I do." He had been married to Gail for many years. She kept him on a fairly short leash, which he didn't like. Though he was in his early sixties, Ken had a full head of jet-black hair, and looked like a man in his forties. He often joked that his remaining goal in life was to retire, but not tell Gail. In that scenario, Ken would leave for work every day, do whatever he wanted to, then return home at six for dinner and TV. Some of us thought he might pull it off someday.

As a self-described alcoholic, and member of AA, he had a ton of stories about his earlier drinking days. Ken wouldn't touch a drop, but when he'd hear some of us talking about how much we'd had to drink over the weekend he'd wait until we finished, then chime in with a story or two about his drinking days, mostly in Chicago. By the time he finished, we younger party animals would feel like amateurs. The stories he enjoyed telling the most were these:

- Ken would begin drinking in midafternoon, head to happy hour with the gang from work, go to dinner, then to a piano bar for after-dinner drinks. Depending on where he was, he'd then try to sleep in a newsstand or other shelter on the street. Why a newsstand? He thought that was his home.
- He wanted to see Eartha Kitt sing, and on at least three occasions he bought tickets at nightclubs where she was appearing. But as she was the headline act, Ms. Kitt would go on last, and by that time, Ken would be asleep at the table, and never did see her perform.
- As a senior executive, Ken would travel on business, often staying overnight in an unfamiliar hotel. One night he and another Y&R executive had been to a long cocktail hour, followed by a long dinner and after-dinner drinks. As they stumbled and taxied back to the hotel, both men managed to lose their hotel keys and had to ask the night clerk for extras. Neither could read the numbers, so Ken asked the clerk what room he was in. "1435, sir," replied the clerk. Ken turned to his partner, and said, "I'll remember the 14, you remember the 35."
- One time after a long night of drinking and eating in Chicago, Ken and a colleague woke up in Las Vegas, not remembering how they got there. They rushed back to Chicago as quickly as possible, arriving in midafternoon, without being seriously missed.

The media director of the Houston office was Ira Tumpowsky, my boss. He had taught me a lot when I had worked for him in New York, and I knew him to be an accomplished media professional, as well as a good leader. He was forceful with his subordinates and clients, but not to the point of being brash or pushy. He was a good family man, with a smart, supportive wife,

Audrey, and three good little boys. As a younger single guy, Ira and I were on different wavelengths socially, but had the same business and media planning philosophies—a lot of that having to do with the fact that Ira had been a major force in my early development as a media planner in New York.

From day one Ira let me carry the ball as far as I could. He made sure I was introduced quickly to Gulf and our other clients. I also met the media reps who called on us from both the local Houston area, as well as the national media reps from Atlanta, St. Louis, Chicago, and elsewhere. Ira gave me as much rope with Gulf as I could handle for several reasons: I established a good rapport with the Gulf clients fairly quickly; I was fully capable of handling their media needs, and there was the temple to build.

The temple had become Ira's passion, hobby, and mission, all in one. When he and Audrey were deciding whether or not to move to Houston from Manhattan, where they had spent their whole lives, they were afraid of prejudice in the south. Even though Texans consider themselves Texans, rather than Southerners, Texas had been part of the Confederacy, and are considered to be Southerners by most Northerners.

Being Jewish, they had fears that even included the possibility that a cross or two might be burned in their yard, especially if they were the first Jewish people in the neighborhood. Upon arriving in Houston they found the population very tolerant, and, in fact, there were two strong temples established there. Ira and a group of his friends decided to start another temple. As one of the founders, Ira became very involved in organizing the new temple, and spent a lot of time on it, including time at the office. Everyone knew about it, and Gene Hart condoned his efforts, as there were important people involved, including some potential clients, and it made for good community relations. The more time Ira spent on the temple, the more he let me carry the ball. He was definitely the media director, and there when I needed him, but I got a lot more responsibility than I would have normally, thanks to the temple.

There were other terrific people at Y&R Houston, and we

were sort of a family. There was "Mother" Marge Homburg, the office manager, who also served as Gene Hart's secretary. Marge was single, had moved down from New York, and had made her work at Y&R the centerpiece of her life. She was a tireless worker, extremely efficient, and reminded me of Miss Hathaway, the bank secretary on *The Beverly Hillbillies*. Marge could be a little pushy at times, but always had the best interests of the staff and the office at heart.

For us single people, she was always trying to find us matches, and in at least one instance was successful: she introduced me to Karen Kessler, who would eventually become my wife. Karen was working as a sales representative for the Sheraton Houston, which was right next door to our office building. In fact, our windows on the fifth floor overlooked the Sheraton Houston's pool on their fourth floor. This provided some nice distractions when certain flight attendants, who stayed there regularly, would sunbathe topless, not realizing that people inside the buildings could see out the mirrored windows, even though the bathers couldn't see in. Karen called on Y&R for Sheraton, and Marge made it a point to introduce us, which ultimately resulted in marriage—more on that later.

Glenn Ashley was a young copywriter who worked for Ken. He was one of the few native Texans in the office, very bright, witty, and articulate. I quickly became good friends with him and his wife Margaret, who worked on one of the upper floors in the same building. We kidded each other about our accents, and they showed me around Houston, eventually introducing me to the beach on Galveston Bay, among other things.

Also in the creative department was Hank Quell, an experienced artist, quiet, efficient, and one who kept to himself. Cezar Miranda was in charge of print production. He and his wife Anna were from Mexico, and introduced me to "Mexican martinis," which were simply margaritas, mixed, shaken, and poured with the ice strained out into a martini glass. No crushed ice, no slush, no sliced lime. Three of those and you were ready for anything.

Tom Allen was the head account man on Gulf Oil, a former

New Yorker, well respected at Gulf. Tom and his wife Nancy spent a lot of time entertaining the head of Gulf's service station advertising, Tom Latimer, who also had a wife named Nancy. We kidded Tom that he had renamed Nancy from Jane or Sue when he had joined the Gulf account team. Sometimes he thought it funny, sometimes he didn't.

Also in account service was Pat Ende, another transplanted New Yorker who worked on Gulf Oil promotions, and Bob Penney, who worked on Gulf Motor Oil. Jim Cameron was an account supervisor on the bank account we had acquired. He was recently divorced, jogged several miles a day to stay in shape, and was considered extremely handsome by most women, which was lucky for him because he liked almost every woman he met.

Several of these guys had moved to Houston while their families remained behind in New York, waiting for the house to sell or school to get out. They all rented a large apartment in Montrose, the bohemian section of Houston. They crudely furnished it with beanbag chairs, several TVs, some tables, mattresses, and two refrigerators—one for beer only. They fancied themselves as swinging bachelors, and referred to their pad as "Dial-a-Hump." As their wives and families gradually moved into Houston, they moved out one by one until "Dial-a-Hump" was cleaned out and abandoned. None of the former residents would say who took the beanbag chairs.

Working with Ira and me in the Media Department was a young man named Phil Kools, who served as the Houston broadcast buyer. Y&R's strategy was to have its branch offices buy all their media locally, as a way to keep involved with the city's advertising and media community, helping to hear about and secure new business. Phil had moved down from New York, and was friendly enough, but kept very much to himself, participating very little in the group functions that went on during and after office hours. He eventually went to work for one of Houston's TV stations, which most of us found strange, as he didn't have a salesman's personality.

Also with us were various secretaries, all of whom were locals, and most of whom came and went fairly quickly. One long-term, outstanding one was Sue Somers, our secretary in the Media Department. She was a sweet, even-tempered Houston flower, who I'm sure found great amusement in watching us Yankees adapt to Texas. Another long-termer was Kay Blackburn, from West Texas. Though she hadn't attended college, Kay was smart and well spoken. That's why I was so surprised when she insisted that she had attended several tent-revival meetings, and seen several "miracles" performed by various evangelists. These included lame people being enabled to walk and someone's foot growing back after being amputated. At first I thought Kay was putting us on, but she was totally convinced that these "cures" had taken place in front of her eyes.

So here we were, twenty or so of us in the growing metropolis of Houston, with a big, prestigious anchor account. Our backgrounds ranged from tough, Brooklyn-born cynics to mild-mannered West Texans who believed in miracles from televangelists. We were a diverse but happy family. It seemed as if we were in our own little world, and in some ways we were. But outside events were about to crash in on us, leading to changes we couldn't have imagined before they occurred.

CHAPTER SEVEN

What Oil Company Conspiracies?

The Y&R Houston family was one that worked hard and played hard. The working side revolved around Gulf Oil, a twenty-million-dollar account that promoted gasoline and motor oil. Like most big oil companies, Gulf spent lots of money trying to convince drivers that its gas was somehow superior to others. Exxon told you their gas was peppier: "Put a tiger in your tank." Shell's gas got you better mileage because it had something called Platformate in it. There were constant promotions by the oil companies, offering steak knives, glassware, or other premiums with a fill-up.

Gulf's commercials ran during space shots, all of which were covered live by all three major TV networks, and on various primetime and sports programming. We also bought sports sponsorships with local teams in major markets. Atlanta was one of Gulf's best markets, and we always had a big deal going with the Braves, even though they were perennial losers. We knew the Braves were owned by some guy named Turner, but there was no TBS, and virtually no cable TV as we know it today. As someone from Gulf said, "Make sure we buy a lot of TV in Atlanta because we spill more down the driveway there than we sell in most markets."

In 1973 the economy was recovering from an earlier economic slowdown. Americans were buying bigger cars that ran on cheap gasoline. It was around thirty cents a gallon in Houston, some of the cheapest in the country. I may have been typical of the thinking on cars and gas at the time. Upon arriving in Houston I bought a brand-new 1973 Mustang with a 351-cubic-inch engine in it. It got only twelve miles to the gallon, but gas was cheap, and there was plenty of it. The days of lavish gasoline advertising, price wars, and premium giveaways came to an abrupt end with the Arab-Israeli War.

During October 1973, the Arabs and Israelis again went to war. The Yom Kippur War lasted only six days, but the repercussions were severe and long lasting. The Arab nations stopped all oil shipments to the United States because of our support for Israel, and the price of oil quintupled, compliments of OPEC. Gasoline became scarce, leading to long lines at service stations, as drivers waited to pay higher prices than they ever imagined. Very quickly the public began looking for someone to blame for the shortages and high prices. The oil companies became the target, and suffered some of the worst public relations fiascoes ever seen.

Gulf and the other big oil companies were accused of acting in concert to create shortages and raise prices. And this sentiment wasn't just from uneducated or uninformed people. Gulf would get threatening notes scribbled on articles and advertisements torn from prestigious publications such as the *Wall St. Journal, New York Times,* and *Newsweek.* Some of these notes were well written, some were from crackpots, some were from semiliterates, but they all expressed their hatred for Gulf and the other "conspirators." Many were threatening, and at one point Gulf had all its mail opened by its security forces, both in its U.S. headquarters in Houston and in its worldwide headquarters in Pittsburgh. We were told that at least two bombs were found in Gulf's mail, but neither went off.

Whichever conspiracy theory was or wasn't true, one thing quickly became clear: For obvious reasons, oil companies could no longer advertise gasoline. Gulf and the other oil companies were under heavy fire from the public, elected officials, and much of the press. They couldn't simply duck and cover, hoping for the crisis to blow over. There was no telling when the situation would improve, as it was out of the control of the oil companies, the American public and the U.S. government, unless it decided to use force to end the embargo, which it didn't do.

The oil companies wanted to try to combat the black eyes they were getting from all sides, and they adopted different strategies to do so. Mobil Oil responded with a long-running series of hard-hitting editorials, taking a combative stance against its accusers. Their PR department, under the direction of Herb Schmertz—who became somewhat of a celebrity in the process—defended everything from the capitalist system to how gasoline was produced. Their editorials ran in publications that reached the all-important "opinion leaders" of the day. Mobil also increased promotion of its sponsorship of *Masterpiece Theater* on PBS. They knew that not many people watched it, but hoped to benefit from public goodwill for underwriting the cost.

Shell Oil published its *Shell Answer Books* that provided safe driving habits, safety maintenance tips, and gas-saving hints. Glassware and steak knife promotions disappeared. Later on Shell committed to sponsoring the *Bicentennial Minutes* on CBS for the two years leading up to July 4, 1976. The minute consisted of a celebrity explaining an event that happened on that particular day two hundred years ago, as the colonies approached their declaration of freedom. This was followed by a brief message from Shell. It was felt by many media professionals to be an extremely smart buy: Shell was on consistently every night in primetime, on different programs, reaching a wide audience, separated from its competitors and in an educational, patriotic environment. People talked about it, late-night hosts parodied it, and it became part of the vernacular for a while.

Gulf began communicating to various target segments in different ways. In an effort to reach "opinion leaders" Gulf began underwriting the *National Geographic Specials* on PBS. They spent fifty million dollars on that project between 1974 and 1984 as an important part of their communication strategy. Separately, we ran some hard-hitting ads, more combative than Mobil's, that responded to specific attacks by politicians or other figures. When Gulf announced its profits for the quarter we ran an ad pointing out that Gulf made only two cents of profit per gallon of gas it sold. Another ad that we produced showed a stereotypical politician, overweight and shifty eyed, pointing an accusing finger at some businessmen. The headline read, "Nothing is so **ineffective** at solving a problem as a pointing finger." This reportedly truly aggravated some senators, who passed the word to Gulf corporate headquarters in Pittsburgh that they had gone too far and should back off. Gulf apparently got the message, and they had us tone down what had been perceived as anti-politician advertising.

Gulf also changed most of its consumer-advertising dollars from promoting gasoline to addressing car maintenance. We looked for people who changed their own oil as targets. Changing one's own oil was not a common thing then, as most service stations would still fill your tank and check the oil. We offered tips on how to maintain your car, especially changing oil. The "Car Care" campaign ran in predominantly male-oriented magazines, including *Time, Sports Illustrated, Popular Mechanics, Field & Stream, Boating,* and *Mechanix Illustrated.*

And in what was a revolutionary move at the time we placed the campaign in a women's magazine. Neither Gulf nor any other major oil company that we knew of had run a sustained campaign in a women's magazine. The thinking then was that "the little woman" might drive the car occasionally—bringing Dad to the train station, dropping off the kids at school or baseball practice—but that men handled the purchasing decisions when it came to new cars, and oversaw their maintenance whether at home or in the shop. But the representatives from *Woman's Day* came to us with a study they had conducted, showing that almost 50 percent of cars going into service stations during the "daytime" hours were driven by women, and that they were even gaining influence in the selection of the family car. Their study, and many later ones, concluded that in most marriages, each partner had veto power over the final selection of a car's make, model, and color—that is, both spouses had to be convinced that a specific car was the one to buy. The study was convincing, and we listened. *Woman's Day* had a feature in each issue that addressed car care from a woman's perspective, and we agreed to run ads adjacent to that feature during the upcoming year. It wasn't that we were pro women's lib, trying to be politically correct, or avant-garde. It was simply a good business decision, and to Gulf's credit, they went along with our recommendation.

And to *Woman's Day's* credit, they did what all media forms do when they crack a new advertising category: they went to all the other companies in that category and merchandised the fact that one of their own was using the medium. Gulf was now advertising in *Woman's Day* and the magazine leveraged it with other oil companies, and even automotive companies, to show them it was "okay" to advertise there. It worked, as it usually does, because so many advertisers have a herd mentality, and once one company in their category uses a medium, the others often follow fairly quickly. *Woman's Day* treated us right after that, remembering that we'd helped them crack at least two big categories.

In addition to some significant changes brought about by the oil shortage, such as reduced highway speeds, there were some relatively inconsequential adjustments that people made as a result of the shortages. There were several big oil company executives in Houston who had ranches far out of town, to which they drove on weekends. The word was that several of them had secretly installed auxiliary gasoline tanks on their cars. This enabled them to travel farther between fill-ups and avoid the possibility of getting stuck somewhere in East Texas with an empty tank.

Besides the crash of big-car sales, there was another casualty of the oil shortage. A forty-foot Gulf Oil sign sat on top of the Gulf building. It had stood there for decades, visible for miles as you approached Houston on any highway, serving as a beacon for "Oil town, USA." The big round Gulf logo was illuminated at night using methane. Some energy savers figured out that the fuel used to illuminate the sign could heat and light fifty homes for a year, and maintained that Gulf was blatantly wasting energy on the sign. After a few months of bad publicity, Gulf decided to take the landmark down, which a few helicopters accomplished one afternoon. It was a highly visible example of how the oil shortage was impacting people in many different ways.

There never were the gas lines in Houston that most of the rest of the country experienced, though sometimes we had to look for an open station. Because so much oil was refined just outside of Houston, there was usually plenty of gasoline to go around. And if we were ever short, there was a gas station on the ground floor of the Exxon building in downtown Houston, just a few blocks from Y&R's offices. Despite our loyalty to Gulf, a few people did switch to Exxon in a pinch.

As this was going on, I was trying to develop a good relationship with the Gulf marketing team. This was fairly easy to do, as they were professional and friendly. They simply wanted good advertising, along with some occasional drinking partners and tennis opponents. As with all clients, one of the services agencies provide is tickets to sporting and entertainment events. Since agencies are connected to those industries, they usually have access to both everyday tickets and those that are hard to get. Early upon my arrival in Houston I was called by one of the Gulf clients with a request that I get him four tickets to the upcoming University of Houston football game. I called our rep at the appropriate radio station and asked if they had any available for Saturday's game. "Oh, sure we do," was the response I got (Gulf was one of the team's sponsors), "how many y'all want?"

"Four would be great," I replied.

"You got 'em," said the rep. "I'll leave them for you to pick up at the GM."

I didn't know what the GM was, so I said, "The GM?"

"Yeah, the main one," he said.

Now I admitted my confusion. "The main GM? What is it?"

He kept his friendly tone, and said, "You know, the main GM, it's right on campus."

Now I was baffled and ready to admit I didn't know what he was talking about, as I was unfamiliar with the University of Houston's campus, and said so. Now he started to sound a little mystified himself, but finally cleared things up when he said again, "You **know**, the GM, where they play basketball."

That was my first real introduction to the language barrier that sometimes separates Northerners from Southerners. My new Southern friends thought it was hilarious.

About this time, Young & Rubicam formed Y&R National, which was to be a chain of offices around the country, designed to serve clients in those areas. The New York office was **not** to be a part of Y&R National, thereby eliminating, in theory at least, potential client conflicts between the Y&R National offices and New York's wide-ranging list of clients. The Y&R National offices were to be located in smaller cities than the traditional advertising centers outside New York—Chicago, Los Angeles, St. Louis, etc. And these offices were to be acquired from local owners, who would be kept on as managers, using Y&R's vast resources and international connections to help them grow.

Y&R's first acquisition was Brewer Advertising in Kansas City. Brewer was a successful agency with several good pieces of business, including a few consumer-oriented accounts, as well as some business-to-business, avionics, and agricultural accounts. Houston was the closest ongoing Y&R office, and was part of the Y&R National system, so we were a logical office to establish liaison with Brewer once it joined the fold. A short time after the acquisition, Gene Hart, our general manager, ordered me to spend a week at Brewer, so as to establish contact with their media department, learn and report on their media procedures, and see where they might be able to tap into Y&R's media resources.

I felt honored to be given this task and did my best to accomplish the mission. I spent an enjoyable, productive week in Kansas City, meeting management, the media department, and some of their clients. They were friendly, hardworking Midwesterners, glad to be part of Y&R, but a little apprehensive of the unknown changes that were to take place. Their media department was well run and competent. My report, written to Gene Hart with a copy to my boss, Ira, was several pages long. I knew it would be sent to New York for review, so I labored over it extensively, knowing it was probably the most important document I had written so far. I was pleased when Gene handed me a copy of it back, with "very informative, good report" written on it. As I said earlier, Gene was a tough grader, and I considered this comment to be high praise from him.

The creation of Y&R National had not impacted us much in Houston. We were still fairly autonomous, dealing with the impact of petroleum sales and marketing resulting from the Middle East situation. Soon after my trip to Kansas City we found ourselves dealing with a situation arising from actions taken closer to home. Y&R, with input from some senior executives at Y&R Houston, purchased another agency in Houston, Rives/Dyke. Rives/Dyke was very much a local Texas agency. It was run and staffed by virtually all Texans, with Texas accounts, most having something to do with oil.

There were several big differences between Y&R Houston and Rives/Dyke, in addition to the fact that Y&R was comprised of mostly Yankees, while R/D was comprised primarily of Texans. The regional differences weren't as big a gap as the business philosophies of the two groups. The main difference was in how our work—media recommendations, creative strategies, and even specific ads—was presented and positioned to our clients.

Y&R's philosophy was to produce the best work we could, then present it to the client as a **strong** recommendation for them to follow. While we listened to their comments, we fought hard to convince them to approve our recommendations, even if they initially rejected it. While we didn't always "fall on our swords" defending every little piece of our work, we would fight hard to convince clients that we were right. This was primarily because we had tons of experience, we had done our homework, and partially because of bravado—we were part of the great Y&R, whose recommendations shouldn't be questioned by clients or anyone else.

On the other hand, R/D would typically present its work to clients and wait for their reaction. If they objected or disagreed with the work, the R/D people were not inclined to strongly defend it. Instead, the attitude was more like, "Okay, we'll come back tomorrow with something different."

Furthermore, Y&R's work was generally presented to clients

by the people in the departments—creative, media, research, etc.—who had done the work. Account Service people most often led those meetings, of course, but the people who had done the work typically presented—and defended—their own recommendations. Contrarily, the Account Service people at R/D typically presented all their agency's work. Sometimes the media, creative, or research people who had done the work weren't even in the meeting. This obviously made recommendations harder to defend, even if the inclination to do so had been there. Typically, if a client didn't like the work R/D presented to them, they'd walk away and come back a few days later with a different recommendation.

These differences, in who should present the agency's recommendations, and how strongly they should be championed, were an underlying basis of ongoing conflict once the merger took place. They were initially papered over by letting the former R/D people continue to deal with their old clients in their manner. Meanwhile, the former Y&R people continued with their procedures. Eventually, Y&R's philosophy was adopted throughout the merged agency, but it took time and a few "come to Jesus" meetings to get there.

At one point Gene Hart sent out a memo to key staff members that "strongly encouraged" everyone to make sure they felt confident about their recommendations to clients, then defend them strongly if challenged. Shortly after that, one of the top creative executives, a former R/D staffer, was pitching an important set of commercials to Houston Natural Gas, which would later grew into Enron. It was an important new campaign, the first major campaign presented to HNG from the merged agencies.

Mr. Creative was pitching his heart out, putting everything he had into it, going on for fifteen minutes with a full-court press. As he wound up his emotional speech he apparently remembered Gene's memo, and ended with a final statement: "We've put more thought and effort into this than any previous campaign we've ever shown you. You're crazy if you don't approve it." It was one of the boldest statements I'd ever heard a creative person say to a client. HNG's people waited for their marketing vice president to react before saying anything. After a moment of reflection, he simply said, "I don't like it." We waited for Mr. Creative to respond, to defend the work, and he did, with these immortal words: "That's okay, we're not **married** to it."

A more urgent and a more open issue that affected the merger was the awarding of titles and division of authority to the staff. Both agencies had a general manager, a creative director, a media director, and so on. The big issue was who would assume these titles within the merged agency. While Y&R was undoubtedly the buyer, and in overall control of the merged agency, the top R/D managers had relationships with their clients, which were really the items that were being purchased. Those people had to be kept happy, including Gerry Black, the majority owner of R/D.

In a diplomatic manner, Y&R Houston personnel were given the titles of creative director, media director, etc. Their R/D counterparts were given the titles of deputy creative director, deputy media director, etc. Gene Hart of Y&R became the CEO of the agency, while Gerry Black of R/D became the COO of the agency. The dance began from there, with the usual office politics taking place within the more complicated merging of two different agency cultures.

Another "incident" complicated the merger, again resulting from the fact that Y&R had purchased an agency in a market where it already had an office. Gulf was a huge, multinational company, one of the biggest oil companies in the world, and proud of it. They were happy to have one of the world's largest advertising agencies as their marketing partner. With the merger, the new agency's letterhead read "Rives/Dyke/Y&R," as opposed to the old "Young & Rubicam Houston." The new letterhead didn't sit well with the corporate egos at Gulf, and they quickly made their objections known. Tom Allen got a call from Tom Latimer, Gulf's director of Service Station Advertising, inquiring if there was any of the old "Young & Rubicam Houston" stationery left. Tom replied that yes, there was, as it hadn't been tossed out yet. "Good," responded Latimer, "use it for all your correspondence to us." When Tom asked why, Latimer said simply, "We hired Young & Rubicam, not something called Rives/Dyke/Y&R. Call yourselves anything you want, but we want to deal with Young & Rubicam." When you're a twenty-million-dollar account, you get to say things like that, so the old stationery didn't go to waste.

For me personally, the merger was working out fine. I still reported to Ira, and continued to have media responsibility for several accounts, including Gulf. As the scope of Ira's responsibilities increased, he gave me even more leeway with my accounts, which I enjoyed. I liked most of the new people in the department and the agency, though we lost the "Y&R Houston family" feeling that had existed. That was only natural, as the twenty of us were joined by fifty R/D people. There were some adjustment pains going on, as each group tried to get used to each other. Some were major, and resulted in some changes in the Creative Department, always known as the most volatile department within agencies. Some were minor. I was in Ken Ventura's office one day, as he picked up his expense account, which had been kicked back to him by the new accounting department. The amount he had spent on gasoline for his company car was being questioned, and he quickly became agitated. "These guys ought to be more concerned about their goddamn accounts instead of ten dollars worth of gasoline," he said vehemently. It was one of the few times I ever saw him show that he was mad, instead of dismissing something with a wry remark.

We moved into the R/D building, which was closer to my apartment on Westheimer Road, as well as my new girlfriend's apartment a few streets away. Add that to the fact that my favorite tennis courts and restaurants were also close by, and my world could have become very small, except for business trips and visits to my parents home in New York a few times a year.

But after a few short months I received a second overture from a major agency in Dallas. I had talked briefly with Tracy-Locke a year or so earlier, but lots of things hadn't been right, and nothing serious happened between us. But in the past year Tracy-Locke had become "hot," picking up the Phillips Petroleum account and more business from one of their longtime major clients, Frito-Lay.

They called me again, and we started discussions. There was a slight misstep on my part early on. Because of my Gulf Oil experience, I assumed they wanted to resume talking because of Phillips Petroleum. But they said, no, they were looking for someone to head up a media planning group with Mountain Bell as the lead account. Wanting to be frank with them, I quickly confessed, "I haven't had any experience with soft drinks." Amused, they replied that Mountain Bell wasn't a soda, but was the telephone system in the mountain states, and that no telephone company experience was needed.

We continued discussions. I flew to Dallas to meet some key people, and we reached an agreement for me to join Tracy-Locke as an associate media director. After five great years at Y&R, it was very hard to go into Ira's office with my resignation letter. Not only had the company hired me right out of school, it had trained me, introduced me to real leaders in the business, and given me major responsibilities on some household name accounts. On the other hand, T-L offered new opportunities and a new city, even though I still liked Houston. And I'd be back in the headquarters office of an agency, though T-L had branch offices in Denver and Houston. Regretfully, I handed Ira my letter, and let him know that it had been a tough decision to make, and that I hoped we could still be friends. I also assured him that if needed, I would stay beyond the traditional two weeks' notice that I was giving. He'd been there before, and took it well, saying that yes, we'd definitely remain friends, and that yes, he'd like me to stay another three weeks to finish up some major plans that I'd been working on. I said I would, and went back to my office to tell T-L that I'd be coming to Dallas a little later than planned.

Ira told Gerry Black that I had resigned, and of my offer to stay on longer than the two-week standard. While not there, I was told later that Gerry was very unhappy and ordered Ira to have me leave at the end of that day, allegedly due to the fact that the agency was competing with T-L for the Texas Visitors Bureau account, and I might compromise their position. This was ridiculous in that I wasn't involved in that pitch and knew nothing about it. But more importantly, out of loyalty to Y&R, I would never reveal anything about it even if I had that kind of information. My feeling is that Gerry Black, as COO and former head of Rives/Dyke, overreacted to my departure because I was the first former Y&R staffer to leave the merged agency. Gene Hart, technically Gerry's boss, chose not to overrule him on this decision, though Ira went to him and requested it.

I felt badly about how my departure was turning out, but the good news was that Y&R agreed to pay me for the following two weeks, even though they were telling me to get lost. It wasn't the Y&R way, but that's the way it was. Though there wasn't time for a going-away party at the office, Glenn Ashley organized one a few days later at one of the nearby saloons. It was a bittersweet occasion, as they say. I remember having a lot to drink, and there was a minimum of speeches and other sentimental verbosity. I did, however, receive the traditional going-away present that was given to almost everyone at these occasions: a bottle of Houston air, which consisted of a jar, half-filled with air and half-filled with water.

CHAPTER EIGHT

A Great "Spokesman" Who Doesn't Speak

The discussions I had with Tracy-Locke were initiated by Larry Spelling, the agency's media director. Larry was an experienced media professional, having been at BBD&O and a few other major New York agencies.

T-L had hired him about a year earlier, as the agency grew and top management realized the media department needed to be upgraded.

The move to improve T-L's media capabilities had been triggered by Larry's boss, Jerry Stevens. Jerry had been one of the top account executives at T-L and was the most vocal critics of the old media department. He was tired of what he considered to be the incompetence of the old guard and wasn't shy about telling anyone who'd listen, including the other members of T-L's top management. His complaints were listened to, but as with many agencies, upgrading the media department was postponed for as long as possible. When most agencies "grow up," they first upgrade the account service and creative departments, then worry about improving the media department. That had been the case with T-L.

But finally, action was taken. Jerry was out drinking with the agency's president, Norm Campbell, one night, and began his laments about the shortcomings of the media department. Through several drinks, Jerry continued the barrage, and finally Norm had had enough. While usually a big, friendly Texan, Norm could be tough when challenged. As related later by Jerry, Norm finally jumped up, and said, "Goddammit, if you think media's so bad, why don't you go down there and run the goddamn department yourself?" Jerry quickly responded, "Okay, goddammit, I will." So that's how Jerry became the acting media director, with the primary task of finding a true media professional to run, train, and grow the department on a permanent basis. After a long search, involving headhunters in New York and Chicago, Larry was selected and a deal was cut. By the time I arrived at T-L, Larry was well on his way to building a first-class media department, and I was anxious to become part of it.

Tracy-Locke was an established Dallas agency, having been formed in 1913. It had been built around the Borden milk business and Dr. Pepper. There was a Mr. Tracy and a Mr. Locke, who devoted themselves to building Dr. Pepper—invented in Waco—into a major soft drink brand. They were so devoted that after many years, when Dr. Pepper fired the agency, Mr. Locke shot himself out of remorse. T-L had grown to a respectable thirty-five million dollars in billings under the leadership of Morris Hite, who now served as chairman of the board, and was a member of the informal yet powerful businessman's group that made the major decisions for Dallas at the time.

Now T-L was run by a triumvirate consisting of Norm Campbell, a big man who fit my image of former Governor John Connally; Bill Boone, another big man who liked to play a semi-educated redneck, but who was as sharp as a tack; and Stewart Michaels, a soft-spoken man who earned the confidence of his clients and demanded the best from those working for him. Norm and Bob were the "outside" team. Stewart worked closely with several of the older, "establishment" clients such as First National Bank in Dallas and the North Texas Commission, a regional business development organization. This was an interesting account to work on, as the commission was populated by such notable personalities as Stanley Marcus of Nieman-Marcus and Charles Tandy, founder of Radio Shack. T-L was one of the three leading agencies in Dallas at the time, the others being the Bloom Agency and Glenn, Bozell and Jacobs. All reported billings of around thirty-five million dollars, but of course we thought T-L was superior.

One of the reasons we thought so was because our client list had a more prestigious list of national companies than our competition. T-L had Borden Dairy & Services, several brands from Frito-Lay, Haggar Slacks, Dole Foods, and Texas Instruments among others. We also had LTV, one of the first conglomerates; Bama Foods, another division of Borden that made jams and jellies; and Wilson Foods, one of the largest meat processors in the country.

At the time, T-L was in a real growth stage. A year earlier it had won the Phillips Petroleum account. I came on board due to the win of the Mountain Bell account. But the real test of an agency is how much it grows internally from its current clients, and on that score T-L was doing extremely well. A few years earlier, T-L had been assigned a new snack food from Frito-Lay named Doritos. It was thought that Doritos would be a nice little regional brand in the Southwest, playing second fiddle to Fritos, Ruffles, and Lay's Potato Chips, the company's big national brands.

But then someone decided to test Doritos—Frito was big on tests—in a few northern markets, just to see what would happen. They were a big hit in those markets as well, and Doritos were rolled out nationally. The commercials featured the comedian Avery Schrieber in situations where someone was trying to execute a delicate task just as he "crunched" a Dorito. Avery Schrieber was used for years, and the brand grew beyond anyone's predictions. In fact, sometime in the midseventies Doritos surpassed Lay's Chips as the leading snack food brand in the country.

A few of the spots became classics as Doritos spent millions on network TV, using Schrieber as the celebrity endorser. He never said anything, but simply "crunched" a Dorito just at the right time to cause a calamity. There was one spot in which a sculptor was about to put the finishing touch on a bust, but as Avery "crunched," the sculpting tool slipped, and the artist cut off the head of his sculpture. Another spot, entitled "Duck Blind," had a group of hunters sighting in on their target, when Avery "crunched" and caused all of them to miss. The most famous spot, and the one with the highest recall score, was where a pool player was about to shoot a delicate shot. Avery was a bystander, and of course "crunched" a Dorito just as the player was about to shoot, causing him to rip a tremendous tear in the table's felt cover with his pool cue.

People often asked why the "crunchiness" of Doritos was emphasized so much, compared to other qualities, such as good taste. The answer lies in the fact that research had shown that the most meaningful attribute of snack foods was freshness and texture, able to be demonstrated by how "crunchy" the snack was. To a majority of people, a "crunchy" snack meant a tasty snack. An earlier campaign for Doritos, based on taste and lifestyle, had misfired. It used the tagline, "The new beat in things to eat," and sales were disappointing. Frito-Lay told T-L to come up with a better campaign, or lose the account.

As the account was about to be taken away from T-L, a copywriter came up with the idea of basing the brand's advertising on its "crunch." The tagline for Doritos became "They taste as good as they crunch," and the ads used humor to convey the message. Avery Schreiber, with his bushy mustache and bushy hair, was chosen as the "spokesperson," even though he didn't speak in the ads. He simply "crunched" a Dorito at the wrong time, using his rubbery face to do the talking. Later on, when Nacho Cheese Doritos were introduced, and became the largest-selling flavor, the tagline was revised to, "The crunch says Doritos, the flavor says cheese." This was a result of more copy research that showed flavor was a big factor with consumers when it came to cheese.

The campaign with Schreiber was so effective and so memorable that it ran for years, and during that time Doritos' sales went from sixty million dollars to six hundred million dollars. And as sales of Doritos grew, the brand's advertising budget grew dramatically as well, with the agency getting a lot of credit from Frito for its success. Frito was so happy with the work that when they came out with another "Southwestern" chip, Tostitos, it gave T-L the assignment. Tostitos was in test markets—northern and southern cities—when I arrived at the agency. The brand eventually rolled out nationally, and has been successful, but not on the level of Doritos.

As one of three media group heads, I reported to Larry, with all the agency's accounts divided between us. Kelly Calhoun was in charge of Phillips, which was an account that had its own dedicated media team. Will Atwater headed up another media group with the Frito-Lay brands as its core. I headed up the third group, which included Mountain Bell. While the Mountain Bell account team and media buyers were in T-L's Denver office, I was to oversee the media planning from Dallas, which meant I'd be traveling to Denver every few weeks. Though I'd never been to Denver, except for an initial meeting with the account service team, I looked forward to traveling to that beautiful city—and I wasn't a skier.

The other accounts to which I was assigned included Bama Foods, a division of Borden, which wanted to be the "Smucker's of the South"; Igloo coolers, in constant battle with Coleman in the cooler and camping equipment categories; LTV, which was concentrating on its aircraft division at the time; the North Texas Commission, formed to bring more business to the Dallas/Ft. Worth area; and First National Bank in Dallas, the largest bank in the city.

Among the people assigned to me were a few that had been palmed off on the new guy—me—by Will and Kelly, the other two media group heads. One in particular, Ernie, stands out as an incompetent misfit who caused problems from the start. He had been poorly trained somewhere else before coming to T-L. He simply didn't have the media knowledge to keep up with the new media department that Larry was building. We could have taught him what he needed to know, and Larry had tried, but Ernie was arrogant and thought he knew everything. He also had a problem with the bottle, which surfaced about the time I arrived.

Larry had warned me that Ernie was on his way to being fired, but wanted to give him one last chance with me to see if he could be turned around. I was willing to give anyone a chance, and Ernie and I had a frank discussion about his status, my expectations, and my willingness to help him improve. He assured me he wanted to stay, and would do his best. I soon saw one of his problems. He missed a deadline on an assignment, so I investigated. It turned out he had seen a Budweiser commercial with a beach scene in which an Igloo cooler had been used. Instead of getting his necessary work done, Ernie had made several phone calls to Budweiser's marketing people and their agency. He was trying to find out if they were going to produce any more commercials that might show a cooler, and if they were, how could we help assure that they'd continue to use Igloo coolers in their spots. He had also written a few follow-up letters to the people he had spoken to. While I thought it was a good idea, the amount of time he'd spent was way out of proportion to the potential benefits. And it was something that the Igloo people or T-L's account service people should handle. It wasn't his job to obtain product placement in someone else's commercial, especially if it caused him to miss a deadline, however minor that deadline was.

The second incident took place one morning when I heard a commotion down the hall from my office. Coming out I saw a group of people around Ernie's office laughing hysterically. It seems Ernie felt sick to his stomach, wasn't able to get to the men's room and had thrown up in his trash can. I quickly determined that he didn't feel bad anymore, so I couldn't fault the others for laughing at someone who was sick. Several of us figured it was the result of a bad hangover. Ernie seemed a little embarrassed, but also seemed to like being the center of attention for a while. I decided to let this incident slide, as there were often hijinks going on within the agency walls that wasted more time than this one had. I put it down mentally as "strike two" for Ernie.

"Strike three" came not too long after that. The head of the accounting department came down with an invoice from a magazine for a full-page, four-color ad for LTV, a client that Ernie worked on. They had no authorization from LTV to pay it, meaning the client didn't ever approve the expenditure. It had been sent down to Ernie a few weeks earlier, and he had confirmed that he had issued an insertion order for the ad, and that it should be paid. But again, LTV refused to pay for the ad, costing about eight thousand dollars, because it was not on the authorization forms that T-L had clients sign before ordering an ad from a magazine or any other medium.

Upon being confronted with this situation, Ernie admitted that he'd gone to a long, wet lunch with the magazine's rep, had come back and ordered the ad without approval from the client or anyone else. He could have canceled the ad the next day, but either forgot to do so, or just figured he'd let it go. This was a scenario that you'd expect to find in a movie, or a nightmare: a smooth-talking rep finagling an ad from an unsuspecting buyer over drinks, except that Ernie wasn't an innocent novice. Without the ad being authorized, even in a publication that was beneficial to LTV, it wouldn't pay for it, causing T-L to lose eight thousand dollars. Something had to be done, so I met with Larry, explained what had happened, and we decided that Ernie had to go at the end of the day on Friday.

Late on Friday afternoon we called Ernie into Larry's office and let him go. He took it fairly well, recognizing that he wasn't working out and would be better off someplace else. He wasn't a terrible guy, and we showed some compassion. It was the first time I'd ever fired someone; it wasn't easy then, and it's never become any easier. I've run across a few people who almost enjoy firing someone, but those are few and far between, and usually have a major personality flaw.

While the act of firing Ernie had gone smoothly, if uncomfortably, there was an aftershock. Upon finishing our session in Larry's office, Ernie asked if he could clean out his desk now, rather than have to return on Monday. It was after 7:00 p.m. by then, and the department was deserted, as it usually was on Fridays. Larry and I told him to go ahead, and we killed time talking in Larry's office. In about half an hour we said our final goodbyes to Ernie and headed for the elevator. Larry and I went up to Vic's, the T-L hangout at the top of the building. Unbeknownst to us, Norm Campbell, T-L's president, was coming down in another elevator that stopped at the fifth floor to pick up Ernie. As friendly as ever, Norm saw him with his load of materials, and said, "Hi, Ernie, taking work home, huh? How's it going?" According to Norm, who recounted the incident to us later, Ernie replied, half-sheepishly and half-sarcastically, "Not too good. I just got fired." The next

Monday a memo went around to the entire staff, mandating that in the future, whenever someone was going to be fired, top management was to be notified in advance.

At T-L we thought we had superior people, attracted by the bigger, more sophisticated clients we had. There was a constant influx of new people—creative, account service, research and media—from the major advertising centers around the country, including New York, Los Angeles, Chicago, and other places. T-L was looking to add top-drawer people with prestigious resumes to impress its clients, especially the newer, larger ones. A prospective employee's "credentials" were very important. For instance, Larry told me at one point that one reason T-L was initially interested in me was the "Y&R" and the "New York" on my resume, along with client names such as P&G and Gulf Oil. It became clear that to a smaller agency, a person's "pedigree" was almost as important as his or her abilities, in that a smaller agency lacked the instant credibility—sometimes justified, sometimes not—given to a big agency with a Madison Avenue address.

And when we found the right person, we'd woo them with the usual salaries and perks, but we also had to show them what a great place Dallas was to live. This was still in the early days of the rise of the Sunbelt, and there were many people hesitant to leave the major advertising centers and move to the Wild West. With T-L doing so well, we could afford to entertain serious prospects fairly lavishly. The night before or after a day of interviewing a group of us would meet the prospect at their fancy hotel and take them to an expensive restaurant for many cocktails and dinner.

Dallas was exploding with good restaurants at the time, and we sampled as many as we could. We had expense accounts that were generous, but not unlimited, and we knew they were scrutinized by the accountants to ensure that they were legitimate. I never knew anyone who cheated or falsified their expense account for personal gain, but we did "play the game" when necessary. We knew that any entertainment expense over one hundred dollars was kicked up to Norm for authorization, and that he might question why we needed to take a mere prospect to such expensive places. To get around this, we'd split the bill into several checks for these types of meals, breaking the amounts down to under one hundred dollars, so as to avoid Norm's scrutiny. If it was a sin, we justified it as payment for spending extra time on company business. We worked hard and played hard, and sometimes the playing and working got mixed together.

The people we hired came from all over the country, and T-L would pay for their move. Moving long distance always produces a good story, such as the movers swooping in and packing everything, including the garbage. Or the moving van gets delayed for a few days, causing the recipients to sleep on the floor, or check into a hotel. Or someone's favorite picture gets lost or damaged. The worst moving experience I ever heard about happened to a media supervisor we hired from a New York agency. John Mulaney came down and started right away, while his wife and three kids stayed in Long Island until the house sold several months later. John had purchased a house in Dallas, sleeping on the floor until the rest of the family and their furniture joined him.

Their van was loaded to the roof with all their possessions, including the family car. The car was driven into the van, then a framework built around it to fit additional things on top of it, including rugs, couches, and tables. On its way to Texas from New York the van was involved in a major accident in Alabama. Tragically, the van's driver was killed, and the van flipped over. It was several hours before the van could be righted. The car fell out of the framework, crushing much of the furniture stored on top of it. Then its oil and transmission fluid leaked out, ruining the carpets and couches. It took the Mulaney family months to recover their losses, but John worked out nicely for T-L.

A successful client meeting was almost always followed by an impromptu party of some kind. So were unsuccessful meetings. One memorable party began in the office following a big meeting with Phillips Petroleum. They had approved the upcoming year's Trop-Artic motor oil campaign, an important milestone that set the stage for soon approving the main corporate image campaign, where most of the ad dollars were spent. About four o'clock, as the

Phillips marketing people were loading into their cars for the airport, a party broke out in the offices of the account executives. Bottles of all kinds of liquor appeared, and word quickly spread around the agency. Those who could leave their work gathered around, and a loud, raunchy celebration was soon underway.

It would have been just another party, except for an incident involving one of the junior account executives on Phillips. Al Summers was a rising star, destined for big things. In fact, he rose high at T-L, then later became president of a television network. But that day Al was celebrating one of his early victories, and he overdid it. He got really loaded and staggered into the men's room to "ride the porcelain cyclone." He passed out, and went unnoticed as the party left the T-L offices and moved to a saloon across the street. Later on, Al woke up and tried to get back into the offices from the hall where the men's room was located. It was now about 10:00 p.m., and the building's inner doors were locked. Al's car keys were also locked in the office, so he had no way to get home. The only thing he could think to do was to call his wife and ask her to come in from the suburbs and pick him up. Needless to say, it wasn't a happy phone call or ride home for Al. After some time had passed, Al would laugh as he recounted the story to us.

While T-L was a large successful agency it wasn't a huge, New York-based agency. Its billings of around fifty million dollars put it in the top three in Dallas, but that was small compared to agencies such as BBD&O, Ogilvy & Mather, J. Walter Thompson, and, of course, Young & Rubicam. And whereas the big agencies had a somewhat arrogant attitude that their recommendations were to be accepted simply because they were so big, that wasn't the case at T-L.

Led by Larry, we in the Media Department put a lot of "sell" into the plans we produced. For example, the target audience for Bama jams and jellies was women eighteen to forty-nine with kids. We used a lot of daytime (9:00 a.m.-4:00 p.m.) television to reach them. At Y&R our plans would have simply stated that we planned to use daytime television as part of the media mix to reach our target audience. But at T-L we'd state that we planned to use daytime TV, then back it up with one or two exhibits, using data from A.C. Nielsen to show how many women eighteen to forty-nine with kids viewed daytime TV, how long they watched, and how much jam they purchased. That's a simple example, used to illustrate the fact that we'd source and back up our statements and recommendations extensively.

We were also mindful of the fact that we were often competing with and being compared to much larger agencies in New York, Chicago, and other markets. For example, we were the agency for Doritos, Tostitos, and some other Frito-Lay brands. Our competition, handling their other brands, were Y&R New York and BBD&O New York. And when T-L won the Phillips Petroleum account, it was from J. Walter Thompson Chicago. And Borden Foods used several other agencies in New York and Detroit for their brands. So we were playing in the big leagues from Dallas, and out of professional pride, and fear of being shown up and losing an account, we made sure our work could stand up to comparison against any of our competitors.

In 1976 we had our work cut out for us. The Pizza Hut account was up for review. The company was still private and owned by the founders, the Carney brothers. It was a tremendously successful company, and their ad budget was huge at the time, somewhere around twenty to thirty million dollars. Winning it would increase our billings by 50 percent, and we were up against two big Chicago agencies, Foote, Cone & Belding and J. Walter Thompson. Pizza Hut had not yet been purchased by PepsiCo, and was run from its headquarters in Wichita, Kansas.

After we got into the finals we celebrated for a while, then went to work. Practically everyone at the agency did some work on this massive new business presentation, including our chairman, Morris Hite, who reviewed and critiqued the dress rehearsal. It was a massive project that took weeks to bring together, following the usual procedure: research, strategies, executions, media plans, promotions, point-of-sale, etc. Everyone worked their ass off on the pitch, while at the same time trying to keep our current clients satisfied, resulting in many late nights and cranky people in the mornings. Another hurdle was the fact that our pitch, to be performed in Wichita, was scheduled for July 5, right after the Fourth of July holiday that was the nation's bicentennial. We knew we'd be working over that weekend, when the rest of the country was celebrating with the tall ships, huge fireworks displays, and cookouts.

As it turned out, we did spend a lot of time in the office over that weekend, but did manage to watch some of the events on TV. We also went through the usual new business routine of changing everything around at the last minute, trying to guess what the client really wants, and everybody second-guessing what seemed like great work the day before. From the media end, our pitch centered on how network TV delivery varies in each local market. We matched network and spot delivery in all major markets to obtain optimum TV weight in key Pizza Hut markets. We did it with a computer model that we developed, with help from our clients at Texas Instruments. This is a simple task now, with the sophisticated hardware and software available, but in 1976 it was breakthrough stuff. We gave it what we thought was a high-tech name: OPTO '76.

On the evening of July 4 the pitch team, consisting of about twelve people, flew to Wichita, and stayed in a hotel near the Pizza Hut offices. We all had a few drinks together, then went into the modest dining room. The mood was reserved, as we knew we were going to make a very important presentation the next day. The drinking was held down to way below our usual levels. The only fun we had that night was when our waiter, a real nerd, made a big show of preparing a Caesar salad at the table. Apparently, the people in the kitchen shared our opinion of him. As he grandiosely went to crack the egg into the giant bowl, he couldn't—someone had given him a hard-boiled egg, which caused him great embarrassment as it crumbled, rather than dripped over the salad. It wasn't a great night for entertainment, but that's all we had, and all we needed, based on our mission the next day.

We all rose bright and early, had breakfast and went over to Pizza Hut. We made our pitch, then had lunch with the Carney brothers. They regaled us with their stories about starting the business, and their firm belief that pizza was not junk food, and in fact, was a nutritious meal. We pitched and schmoozed hard, but in the end, we didn't win the business. It went to Foote, Cone & Belding, as we were told a few days later. Whether they were trying to make us feel good or not, Pizza Hut told us we finished second, which is about as good as holding the second best hand in poker. Naturally, we felt deflated when we got the word, but nevertheless felt as if we'd given it our best shot, and wouldn't have done anything different. And as it turned out, there was a silver lining to the cloud of rejection: the management of Pizza Inn, headquartered in Dallas, heard about our pitch and invited us to show it to them, as it contained a lot of valuable information about the pizza business. T-L agreed to a meeting, which went well, and Pizza Inn hired us shortly thereafter. Their budget was significantly smaller than Pizza Hut's, but they were a good client for many years.

One of the best things about Pizza Inn was that they were just forming a franchisee advertising co-op organization. We got in on the ground floor, working closely with both corporate marketing people and the franchisees, who had elected an advertising committee to represent them. We attended the meetings, and helped them get their marketing plans and advertising campaign going. The meetings were long and boisterous, as the inherent friction between corporate personnel and franchisees came into play. As the senior media person on the doomed Pizza Hut pitch, it was logical for me to lead our media efforts on Pizza Inn. It was a fun account, as everything was new, with no "here's how we did it last year" attitude, and interesting personalities vying for control over the process.

We worked hard creating the first big campaign for Pizza Inn, which was to be presented to them at their annual franchisee meeting the following February. As luck would have it, Pizza Inn had booked an ocean liner for their meeting—the *Flavia* of Costa Lines—and invited key members of the agency who worked on their business to come along. We'd leave from Miami, cruise for a week with the corporate people and all the franchisees, and present the new campaign to them. The ship had a casino, we'd be cruising to Nassau in February, and all expenses were paid. We figured this was payback for our work over the bicentennial holidays.

We got all the elements of the new campaign together—the new TV commercials, the research results, and the media plans—and headed to Miami. At the time, I didn't know it would be my last business trip for T-L.

CHAPTER NINE

Debbie Does Bartlesville

Tracy-Locke was considered a "strategic-oriented" agency, meaning it was known for the ability of its account service department to provide clients with sound positioning strategies and other marketing advice. Though it had good creative people, it was not known as being creative driven, as many successful agencies are labeled. The three strong personalities that ran the agency all had backgrounds in account service. This made it difficult for the three creative directors who reigned during the four years I was there. Creative directors like to have a lot of control over their departments, if not the entire agency. But they weren't given that control at T-L, so it made for a rocky relationship between T-L's management triumvirate and whoever happened to be creative director.

The three who passed through were all strong, experienced, and talented, meaning they also had big egos and wanted control. When they weren't granted that control, tension grew, ultimately resulting in the creative director leaving, due to their unhappiness with the situation. The triumvirate's philosophy was, "We hired you, you work for us, and when push comes to shove, you're going to do it our way." Since the triumvirate—Norm, Bob, and Stewart—were all involved with clients, especially the major ones, the clashes came more often than if the top guys had used a "hands off" style of management.

The typical pattern was that the new creative director would be announced with much fanfare, both to clients and the agency. There would be a honeymoon period, when the creative director and the triumvirate would get along famously, present campaigns to current clients and pitch new ones, all accompanied by a lot of late-night strategy sessions and drinking. One of the creative directors couldn't quite keep up with the drinking prowess of the rest of the agency. Luckily, he had built up some loyalty with his subordinates in the creative department, who were kind enough to carry him out of several office parties after the drinking had gotten the best of him.

After the honeymoon period came the struggle, when one or more members of the triumvirate would question the creative product, either a specific piece of copy or an entire campaign. Typically, the creative director would begin to defend and fight for the campaign, and possibly get into a protracted argument with the opposing manager. These would multiply in number and intensity over time, with neither party giving in. But the triumvirate was in control, not about to leave, so the creative director would ultimately resign and move on.

My contacts with the creative directors were usually limited to seeing them in presentations, at parties, and up at Vic's, the saloon at the top of the T-L building. I found them interesting, highly egotistical, and not particularly friendly, even over a drink. Their attitude toward media people was that we were lower on the food chain than they were, and we were to be tolerated as a necessary evil to make sure their ads got on the air properly. As a department, we got along fairly well with the creative directors, but our relations were better with the other members of the creative department. We'd party together at office functions, and worked in tandem with them planning campaigns. But we weren't real close to them socially. When it came down to it, we were happy with alcohol as our stimulant, while many of them preferred something different.

Speaking of parties, we had them often, and for any reason we could think of. Winning a new piece of business or getting approval for a campaign qualified. Advertising people are party people, so birthdays, weddings, and babies were all reasons to celebrate. Clients in town also served as an excuse for a party, and the marketing people from Phillips Petroleum obliged us frequently.

Phillips was headquartered in Bartlesville, Oklahoma, a town of about thirty thousand where it ruled just about everything. It was a nice town, but limited in entertainment opportunities. The Phillips people looked for reasons to visit and meet in Dallas, and with their twenty-five-million-dollar budget, we were more than willing to accommodate them. Besides, they were our type of people, in that they liked to work hard, then play hard.

The Media Department had its own entertainment budget for Phillips, which had two media managers that we interacted with. As opposed to the procedure at many agencies, we often met without account service executives being present. The senior media manager, Jeff Dillon, had been with Phillips for many years, and had worked his way up the ladder to media manager. He was smart, knew the oil business, but had never worked at an agency. He would give an order and expect the agency to jump through hoops, often with an unreasonable deadline. But we'd jump through those hoops and meet the deadlines—twenty-five million dollar budgets make those things happen.

Overall, we liked Jeff, but after a few drinks he'd get semibelligerent and throw his weight around. For the most part, he wasn't bad, but part of his third-to-fourth drink routine was to criticize the agency, pointing out our shortcomings, which we felt was nitpicking, but which we usually took in stride before moving on to other topics. But one night, later than usual, Jeff began his criticisms, more adamantly and for a longer period of time than usual. Jerry Stevens, who oversaw the media department as part of top management, had come along that night, and grew angry as Jeff continued his unfavorable evaluations of us, which at one point moved into the area of T-L's creative work. Jerry had had a few as well, and he finally jumped up and said, "Goddammit it, Jeff, if we're so bad, and you're so goddamn important, why don't you just fire us?" Jeff was taken aback by someone standing up to him so forcefully, knowing he wasn't in a position to fire T-L. He immediately backed off, saying we had taken his position all wrong, and that he was just trying to be helpful. It was a happy moment for us media folks, and embarrassing for Jeff. We went with the flow, saving our congratulations for Jerry until the next day, and not piling on. Someone suggested another round, and the evening went on. Jeff's bluff had been called, and for some time after that he toned down his criticism of the agency, eventually going back to his routine, but not when Jerry was around.

A few months later I witnessed another incident with Jeff that convinced me that he liked to beat up on people who couldn't fight back. Several of us were having after-dinner drinks in a decent restaurant with very dim lighting, and we were being served by a nice young waitress. A minute or two after being served his second after-dinner drink, Jeff irately called the waitress to our table, and in front of everyone, held up his rusty nail and asked angrily, "What do you call this thing floating in my drink?" Sure enough, there was a dark piece of material in his drink, which the waitress quickly took back while apologizing profusely. Jeff was not gracious as he handed her his drink. A few minutes later the waitress returned with a new drink, which Jeff accepted with a "well now, that's better" attitude. After she had put down his drink, the waitress put something else down on the table next to it, and said very sweetly, "Sir, this is what was in your drink." Jeff picked up a small, rectangular piece of fabric, and we all leaned in to look at it. "I believe it's the label from your tie, sir," she continued, as polite as ever. Sure enough, Jeff flipped up his tie, and we all saw the label was indeed missing. Further examination showed the fabric to be a label from some unknown tie store. We all laughed, and started giving Jeff a hard time. He let the waitress off the hook, but not with a touch of humor or apology. He seemed embarrassed, but also a little miffed that he had "lost" a confrontation.

One time we had the opportunity to get back at Jeff, and we took it. He had visited T-L for a few days of meetings and was getting ready to head for the airport when he spotted the agency's videotape copy of *Debbie Does Dallas*, the hard-core porn movie that we kept around. He asked if he could borrow it, and Larry said, "of course." Jim stuffed the tape into his suitcase and left to catch his plane. The next day, when Jeff made his daily 8:00 a.m. call to Kelly Calhoun, the associate media director who was in charge of the media for Phillips at T-L, his first words were, "the damn airline lost my luggage." This didn't seem important to Kelly until Jeff went on to lament that the *Debbie* tape was inside it. The conversation went on to the Phillips media business, and the tape was forgotten until later in the morning when Kelly mentioned in a meeting that Jeff's luggage and the tape were lost. Several people seemed to have the same idea at the same time. "Let's not let this opportunity go by," one said. "There's something here," said another. It was decided that Kelly would call Jeff back later in the morning with the distressing news that the luggage and tape had been found at the airport and turned in to the FBI. The story would continue that the FBI had called T-L, looking for the owner, getting ready to charge him with "interstate transportation of pornographic material." The line to Jeff would be, "But don't worry, we'll protect you."

Kelly called Jeff later in the morning, and relayed the message that "the authorities" had the tape and were looking for Jeff. Of course, all this was absurd, but Jeff bought it and sounded scared. Several of us listened to Kelly's side of the conversation and broke into hoots of laughter when he hung up. We decided to wait until the end of the day, then call Jeff and let him off the hook. Our little joke ended in midafternoon, however, when Jeff called and said that his luggage, including the tape, had been returned to him. He laughed, admitted that our plot had scared him, but conceded it had been a good joke. We had to admit that Jeff had handled the situation well, and that overall he was a good client.

In the Media Department we were always looking for ways to plan and place media more effectively than just running commercials or placing magazine ads for our clients. Led by Larry, we were able to do this on an ongoing basis. One strategic accomplishment that we made was for Phillips Petroleum. Headquartered in Bartlesville, Oklahoma, it was a "heartland" company when it came to selling gasoline and motor oil. Their marketing area was the middle portion of the country, leaving out the East and West coasts. We wanted to buy network TV that way, so as to match the network coverage with the Phillips marketing area, but the networks were reluctant to sell anything but the entire country.

If pressed to break up the country, the networks would usually sell the West Coast (Pacific time zone) separately, as network programs, along with their commercials, were actually fed three hours later than on the East Coast. Getting them to break off the East Coast was harder, as there wasn't a "natural" time zone break, because the Eastern, Central, and Mountain zones were all fed at the same time. Through Larry's connections with senior management at the networks, we were able to get their agreement to sell Phillips their "heartland" territory, subject to finding "matching partners," advertisers who would agree to take the East and West Coast feeds that we didn't want. Those partners were easily found, especially after CBS set up an office, run by a veteran sales rep, Marty Slater. He found matches for Phillips and other network advertisers who wanted to buy network TV on a regional basis. Being able to buy regional network TV provided Phillips advantages over buying local TV to cover the same areas: better audience efficiencies, wider coverage, and in-program placement of the ads.

With our success in regional network TV, we began to explore the possibility of doing the same thing with the network radio we bought for Phillips. This was met by unanimously strong "no way" responses by all the major radio networks, of which there were only four at the time: ABC, CBS, NBC and Mutual. We refused to take no for an answer. When Mutual finally said they'd consider selling us their network regionally, we stretched their stance a bit, and told the other networks that Mutual had agreed, and would therefore receive a huge percentage of Phillips' network radio budget. On hearing this, the other networks agreed to sell to us regionally, and we were in business.

For another client, Korbel Champagne, we made a tactical change to their media plans. Korbel, like most champagnes, achieved over 60 percent of its sales in the fourth quarter, for obvious reasons. And the airwaves were cluttered with champagne ads from every producer who could scrape together enough money to put together a campaign. We convinced Korbel to save its limited advertising dollars until the fourth quarter, when we'd put all of it into television. Furthermore, we'd put it all into one daypart—Late Night—that reached an audience that we knew was a good one for partying and purchasing champagne. Finally, we concentrated all our money on *The Tonight Show Starring Johnny Carson*.

We used an opportunity the show offered to new advertisers: if a new sponsor bought a reasonable schedule on the show, and paid for a sixty-second announcement on its first night, Johnny would introduce the product live. Right after his monologue he would hold up the product and welcome it as a sponsor. Our night arrived, and as we hoped, Johnny messed up Korbel's name, then repeated it correctly, joked that Ed McMahan wanted several cases, while showing the bottle the whole time. That kind of endorsement was worth ten times what we paid for it. On top of that, a tape of Johnny's endorsement was played at Korbel sales meetings, distributor meetings and otherwise used as a sales tool. That year, and for several more, Korbel reported to us that they sold every case they produced.

Another client we had was Weed-Eater. These days, virtually everyone with a yard has one, but in the late seventies they were a new tool, enabling people to trim their lawns faster and easier than with the old-fashioned clippers. The Weed-Eater was invented by a man in Houston with a big yard, full of trees. He got tired of constantly trimming the grass around the trees. One day he was going through a car wash and noticed that the car was being cleaned by nylon strings on a rotating cylinder. He thought the same device, much smaller, could twirl the nylon strings at a higher speed and cut the grass around his trees. Using a motor from an electric blender, he made a crude grass trimmer, then made a handle from a broomstick. It worked like a charm, and he built a small assembly plant and started to turn out hundreds of copies.

He sold them from the back of a pickup truck until business got so good that hardware chains and garden stores began carrying Weed-Eater. Sales continued to go through the roof, and the brand needed an ad agency to produce a national campaign. T-L won the account and we were in the yard care business, along with our Poulan chain saw client. In fact, Weed-Eater and Poulan chain saws eventually became sister companies under the Emerson Electric Corporation.

We positioned Weed-Eater as the greatest new piece of yard care equipment since the lawn mower. All the ads showed big, beautiful lawns with large trees, perfectly manicured, along with a beauty shot of the Weed-Eater itself. At one point some letters came into the company, asking if the product could cut human legs or hands. The company got special permission from the right people and conducted tests on cadavers. They showed that yes, the nylon strings would cut skin, but were not capable of cutting off a limb, or even a finger or toe. That was good news—the level of safety warnings could be cut back.

There was no HGTV then, and very little programming about gardening—cable wasn't a factor—so we placed the TV advertising in sporting events, to reach the men who did the "heavy" yard work. We also wanted the buyers and managements of the hardware and mass merchandiser chains to see that the brand was being supported by advertising, a common practice among most brands. In print, we had a wide variety of magazines to choose from: *Better Homes & Gardens, Southern Living, Sunset, Yankee, Old Farmer's Almanac* among others. Weed-Eater went on to become a huge success, and is still the "Kleenex" in the string trimmer category.

At the same time we were working on these accounts, there were interesting things happening at T-L. Because of having so many clients, and looking for opportunities for them, we ran into a wide variety of different people. One instance was hooking up with Frank Bresee, whose company sold time and gave away prizes on quiz and game shows, such as *The Price is Right* and *Concentration*. Frank was a friend of Monty Hall. In fact, the first *Price is Right* had been filmed at Frank's house. Frank knew one of the T-L account execs from earlier West Coast days, and he came to Dallas to solicit business from us. He stayed a few days and brought his current wife, who was considerably younger than Frank, and looked like the model and aspiring actress she was. Several of us had meetings with him by day, then joined him for dinner at night. Frank had a million stories about Hollywood stars, stuff that the tabloids would kill for. While I'd like to repeat a few of his stories here, few of them are flattering to anybody, and all of them are hearsay, so I'll let the tabloids dig up their own dirt. Another thing we liked about Frank was the fact that he had invented a drinking game called *Skip and Go Naked*, a cross between strip poker and several drinking games. He gave all of us a copy, which many of us displayed prominently in our offices for several months after he left, though I don't remember any of us actually playing it.

While all this was going on, my personal life was going through big changes. To this day, when I talk about Dallas, I tell people it's where I got my first wife, had my first child, and bought my first house. And, I'm quick to add, I still have two out of the three. When I left Houston, Karen Kessler left her job at the Sheraton Houston and came with me. Shortly after we arrived in Dallas we got married. Two years later, in 1977, we had our first child, Doug, who came out screaming, and hasn't stopped since. And about that time we moved into our first house in north Dallas, on a nice little street named Princess Lane.

Nineteen seventy-seven seemed to be the year of the babies. My boss, Larry, had his first, as did a fraternity brother, Tom, who was up in New Jersey. I was named godfather to his son Scott, and we named Tom and his wife Marianne as Doug's godparents. My main tennis opponent, Roger Tremblay, was the manager of the *Southern Living* office in Dallas. We'd play tennis at least once a week after work, no matter how hot, then head to a bar to replenish our precious bodily fluids. One night, after our second drink, Roger said he had something to tell me, and I said the same. He went first, and told me his wife, Judy, was expecting in about seven months. I said so was Karen, and we joked that we must have been at the same Christmas party, which we later determined was true. We had several more drinks in celebration and vowed not to let our new arrivals keep us from playing tennis as much as we had been. We kept that promise. Doug and Darren were born a week apart, and within a month Roger and I had them in bassinets at courtside as we bashed the ball back and forth, checking on them each time we changed sides.

And speaking of tennis, I had become a pretty good player with all the time I spent at it. My reputation as a player had apparently spread around the agency, and one day Stewart Michaels invited me to play. I knew about "client golf" and "boss tennis," and didn't like playing either one. As we approached the court, however, Stewart put my mind at ease by telling me that he didn't believe in them either, and wanted me to play as hard as I could. So I did, beating him 6-1, 6-2. He had a good game, but I was younger and played more often. We played a few more times during my career at T-L, and I enjoyed getting to know Stewart better, though we never became drinking buddies, due to the differences in age and professional status. It may have been my imagination, but in our business dealings, Stewart seemed more respectful of my work on his accounts and joked around with me a little more than most other members of the media department.

Toward the end of 1978 a couple of incidents led to a famous comment from our president, Norm Campbell. The Dallas Cowboys were having tremendous success with their great teams of the seventies, led by Roger Staubach. CBS often chose them as the premier game of the week, covered by their top play-by-play team of Pat Summerall and John Madden. The Cowboys were also getting into the playoffs and the Super Bowl regularly. That season a December playoff game was being televised nationally from Cowboy Stadium. True Cowboy fans maintained that they didn't put a roof on the stadium so God could watch His favorite team play. During the game, a fan caught on fire, as his snowsuit was ignited by a hibachi stove he had brought into the stadium. This was caught on camera and replayed several times, though luckily the fan wasn't seriously hurt. It became a highlight of the game, and got a lot of coverage, both nationally and in the Dallas media. It turned out that the chef in the snowsuit was an executive at a competing ad agency, which continued to be mentioned in the press reports.

At about this same time, Dallas police captured the "friendly rapist." This jerk would tie up his victims with a phone cord, rape them, then admonish them not to leave their doors unlocked. Hence, the oxymoron, "friendly rapist." After his capture, it turned out that he, too, was an executive at another competing ad agency. On hearing this in a meeting, and realizing another agency would be getting a lot of ink, Norm jokingly thundered, "Can't **we** get some publicity in this town?"

Some people may think a comment like that, even joking, wasn't "politically correct." Whether it's "PC" today may be debatable, but back then there were a lot of things being done on a regular basis that today would bring reprimands, or possibly even legal action. Language, gestures, comments, and actions that you can't get away with today were commonplace in the seventies. Many of us at T-L engaged in some of these actions, primarily suggestive comments, meant to be funny, which were simply expressions of friendship and admiration for one another, but today might be considered offensive. They ranged from the totally innocent practice of many Southern men calling women "Hon" (as in Honey) or "Sug" (as in Sugar) to other behavior that could definitely be called sexual harassment. At the most innocent end of the spectrum, women in the department would accept what was dished out and dish it back. But when some balked at the extreme end, they found little sympathy. Some of them also had a double standard. For example, there was one beautiful media planner who would cringe when someone used the "F" word in front of her, and would object to its use. At first we tried to respect her wishes, but then a few of her friends told us the "F" word was one of her favorites when she was with them. After that we began using it in front of her as often as possible, and just laughed at her faked shock and horror.

Another incident about this time probably would have meant trouble for the perpetrators today. We hired a media planner named Lane from another city, which turned out to be one of our mistakes. She came with good credentials, but during the interview process got mixed reviews. We should have passed her up, but the ones that liked her were strongly in her favor, and we needed people.

We compromised by hiring Lane, but didn't pay for her move to Dallas from St. Louis. She arrived, went to work, and did a decent job, but quickly became an unabashed Bible beater. Lane recruited four or five other women in the department to conduct Bible studies every Wednesday at noon in one of the department's conference rooms. This was occurring just at the time when Jim Jones was murdering nine hundred of his religious followers in Guyana by forcing them to drink Kool-Aid spiked with poison. In an effort to disrupt the proceedings one Wednesday, several of us mixed up a batch of Kool-Aid and had it delivered to the conference room during their meeting.

Another unfortunate hire we made was a senior planner from an agency in New York. Fred Roth was in his midtwenties, smart, and athletic looking, and very attractive to women. We hired him to work on Phillips Petroleum, and he was performing well. Fred had a girlfriend up in New York, who came down every few weeks, and they talked about getting married sometime in the future. But Fred seemed to be in no hurry, especially after he saw the available women in Dallas. And they liked what they saw, as well.

Fred began going to discos and parties almost every night. He'd have stories for us every day, and as we were married guys who didn't travel in those circles anymore, Fred's stories held our rapt attention. No sense in going into detail here, as any reader can well imagine the subject, and most of the details. Suffice it to say that Fred was very tired most of the time, though he did manage to put in a decent day's work.

Unfortunately, all his partying caught up to him at the wrong time. He and his planning group spent several weeks preparing an important plan for Phillips' motor oil brand, Trop-Artic. Fred was burning the candle at both ends, and the day of the presentation arrived. The T-L group flew to Bartlesville to present the plan to the Phillips marketing people, but first had lunch in the main dining room, where the top executives ate. Whenever we visited it was always interesting to eat there. During the meal, the Phillips custom was for each host to introduce his or her guests to the entire room, giving their name, affiliation, and background. More often than not, a sheik, oil minister, or some other dignitary from the Middle East would be in attendance, with a large entourage, all in their traditional robes. They were all introduced, and we found it amazing that we'd be sitting in the middle of Oklahoma, dining with powerful figures from an oil-rich country from so far away. It was something you never got used to.

After lunch, the T-L and Phillips executives met in the typical surroundings—lots of executives in a large conference room with several TV monitors and an overhead projector. The room would go from light to dark, then light again, as various members of the T-L team gave their part of the presentation. While not an exceptionally large lunch, when combined with Fred's lifestyle, it had a terrible effect. After a period of someone presenting from an overhead projector, the lights were snapped on, and there was Fred, fast asleep in his chair, head tilted back, mouth open wide. The only good thing was that he wasn't snoring or drooling. In another place, at another time, it might have been funny, but in this instance it was definitely not. T-L's management people were embarrassed, and the Phillips folks were not amused. Shortly after the return to Dallas, Fred was told his services were no longer needed at T-L.

One of the many ads for Phillips that T-L produced in this era of gasoline shortages involved a paperboy. It was a corporate ad, promoting the free-enterprise system, which the management of Phillips Petroleum supported strongly. It was part of the effort to show that Phillips was a strong, innovative company, able to develop products that benefited society **because** of the free-enterprise system that existed in the United States. The commercial opened on a paperboy riding his bike, throwing newspapers onto porches and lawns in a nice suburban neighborhood. The voiceover said, "This is an American paperboy. He makes more money than half the people in the world." It was a shocking statement that Don Carlton, the management supervisor on the Phillips business, told me was untrue. "Untrue?" I repeated, "We're going to run false advertising?" "It's untrue," Don replied, "because the average American paperboy makes more than **70 percent** of the world's population. But research showed us that people wouldn't believe it, so we cut it down to 50 percent."

After a few years at T-L I realized something about my abilities and career development. Both Y&R and T-L had taught me a lot about media planning and buying. Y&R had given me a good knowledge of the basics, and an appreciation for the fact that relations between agencies and the media were two-way streets. Both should work together for the benefit of the client. And whereas the power of the mighty Y&R helped propel our recommendations past clients, we didn't have that luxury at T-L. T-L was smaller and didn't have a Madison Avenue address, so clients were more skeptical of our recommendations. They had to be persuaded that our plans were right for their products. To put it simply, Y&R taught me the media basics and philosophies, while T-L taught me how to "sell" a media plan, not with deception, but with solid logic and backup references. I was beginning to feel that I was an accomplished media professional, having been trained and mentored by true professionals such as Ira Tumpowsky at Y&R, and Larry Spelling at T-L.

CHAPTER TEN

How to Become a Campbell Kid

My decision to leave T-L wasn't due to any dissatisfaction with the people or the job itself. For a long time I had wanted to try the client side of the business, and decided to do so if the right opportunity presented itself. I had decided that I would not actively seek an opportunity with a client, but that I would keep my eyes open for one that met my criteria: it had to be a leading, well-known consumer advertiser, **not** located downtown in a big city, and preferably located on the East Coast. I didn't make a list of target cities or companies, nor did I talk to the many headhunters that we used in New York to recruit our talent at T-L.

I did keep an updated resume on hand, ready to use when the right opportunity came by. I was in no rush, as I was happy at T-L. We were a good department, one that had matured and gained the respect of clients and the media representatives who called on us. We therefore received more than our share of calls from headhunters, looking to lure us away. As a sidelight, a prospective client was once evaluating T-L as a place to put a big brand, and we supplied him with our backgrounds, playing up the prestigious organizations we'd come from. This particular prospect then threw us a curve, asking to see where the people who had left the agency in the past two years had gone. We got the account.

At one point I interviewed for the top media job at the Southland Corporation, most famous for owning the 7-Eleven chain of convenience stores. The company was definitely a leader in its field, and with headquarters in Dallas, we wouldn't have to move. The atmosphere didn't feel right to me, and I was concerned that it was a one-product company, with a retail orientation, so we didn't dance together for very long. It wasn't all one sided, however, in that Southland didn't exactly come running after me, begging to continue the dialogue. It was one of those times when two parties are somehow introduced, and quickly determine that they're not right for each other. As in dating, it makes things a lot easier if both parties come to that conclusion quickly.

A few months later I was reading *Advertising Age* and scanned the "help wanted" pages. I immediately noticed an ad for a senior media position at the Campbell Soup Company in Camden, New Jersey. Campbell met my criteria for possibly moving: It was definitely a leading advertiser, always in the top one hundred spenders; it wasn't located in a major city—though near Philadelphia—and it was definitely on the East Coast, being forty-five minutes from the Jersey Shore. I ripped the ad out and made a mental note to follow up on it. About that time we were deep into developing some national plans and test markets for Tostitos, another Frito-Lay brand that was destined to become huge, and I didn't have an opportunity to follow up on the Campbell ad. When things quieted down a little after several weeks, I came across the ripped-out ad, figured the job had been filled, and tossed the ad out. A few weeks later, I got a call from a New York headhunter, Karly Cannon, asking if I'd be interested in talking about a "senior media position with a major food company." As we went further down the road, it became apparent that she was representing Campbell Soup, and I was excited about the opportunity. Karly asked me to send her a resume, which I did. Soon after that, we were in discussions, then the interviewing process.

The process was conducted very formally, very slowly, and very deliberately. This was different from the process at the agencies where I had interviewed, which tended to be less formal and take less time than the Campbell routine. One of the reasons for that was that big companies want to avoid hiring mistakes, in that in our litigious world, it's harder and potentially more dangerous legally to fire someone later. Ad agencies, being smaller, and not as visible to the public, are at less risk in this area.

Another reason that big companies take more time in hiring is that they're not under such pressure in replacing someone as quickly as agencies are. Big companies have assets, such as machinery and trucks, to do some of their work, whereas agencies have only people to turn out their work. When they're short a person, it's the same as a machine breaking down, and it needs to be replaced quickly, so that "production" levels can be maintained. Many agency managers go into a semipanic when someone leaves, and they often move someone up internally, who may or may not be ready. Or sometimes they aren't as discerning as they should be in hiring an outsider. One lesson I learned over the years was to take more time to find the right person for the job, instead of trying to fill it quickly. In the long run, the extra work needed from myself and others to fill the gap is worth it, rather than going through months of agony with the wrong person, then the unpleasantness of having to fire that person.

Campbell was certainly in no rush to fill a chair. By the time Karly the headhunter contacted me, the job had been open for over two months, and they were looking at several candidates. After sending Karly my resume, she wanted to see a few samples of media plans that I'd written. We had several long phone conversations. It was obvious she wanted to be sure of my qualifications before she served me up to someone at Campbell's. She finally became confident enough to do that, and a meeting was set up in New York in January of 1979.

At that meeting, in Karly's offices, I met Bob Bolte, Director of Advertising Services at Campbell. Bob was an experienced media professional who'd worked at several big New York agencies before moving to the client side at Gillette in Boston. He'd been hired by Campbell a few years earlier to lead the media portion of Campbell's marketing juggernaut. He grilled me in a serious manner about my media experience and knowledge. We talked about the differences between being on the agency side of the business compared to the client side, and I could see he was evaluating my ability to direct agency people from the outside, rather than manage them from the inside. I passed, and it became the first of several intense interviews I'd have on my way to beautiful downtown Camden.

A few weeks later I flew from Dallas to Campbell's headquarters, known as the "General Office," or "G.O." I had passed Bob's review and was due to meet with Herb Baum, Director of New Products; Tony Adams, Director of Marketing Research, and a few other people. My schedule for the day was printed out, and the times were to be followed precisely. I later learned at Campbell that all meetings started at the scheduled time, regardless of who was running late. The meetings went well and were fairly routine until I met with the vice president of Human Relations, Ron Hall.

Ron was in his late fifties, and had been at Campbell's for almost three decades. He was the most insightful interviewer I'd ever met, before or since. He was a true "personnel" professional, and was like a psychiatrist in the way he asked very probing, open-ended questions. He started by asking me, "What do you know about Campbell's Soup?" I had done some background work, and told him, "I know that Merrill Lynch says Campbell's is going to earn one dollar a share this year." For better or worse, I got the impression he hadn't heard that response to an opening question before. He continued asking questions, including the age-old, "Where do you want to be five years from now?" But then he continued with several others that really caused me to think:

> "How successful are you?"
> "What would make you quit a job you liked?"
> "Explain the job you're interviewing for, and pretend I know nothing about advertising."
> "If you get it, how do you want to be evaluated in this job?"
> "What is your current boss saying in his annual evaluation of you?"
> "What will your boss be saying about you a year from now, if we hire you?"
> "How do you think your boss on this job should be evaluated?"
> "Are you honest?"

"What would you bring to the job that nobody else will?"
"Why do you want this job?"

Throughout the questioning, Ron was friendly and relaxed, and I felt at ease with him. The questions he asked reminded me of one that a psychiatrist, a friend of my parents, had asked me when I was about fifteen years old: how are a coffee cup and a doughnut alike? There were no apparent "right" or "wrong" answers, but whatever I responded was giving him insight into whatever he wanted to find out about me.

While friendly, Ron was noncommittal, as was Bob at the end of the day. Exhausted, I boarded the plane and flew back to Dallas to await their decision. The next day I got a call from Karly the headhunter, saying that I had done well, but no decision was going to be made for a few days.

In a few days, several of us, including our spouses, were due to attend the annual Pizza Inn franchisee meeting. This was to be aboard the Costa Lines T.S.S. *Flavia*. The day before we left, I called Karly and told her I'd be unreachable for several days, as we were sailing from Miami to the Bahamas aboard the *Flavia*, where exorbitant rates made the radiotelephone too expensive to use, except for emergencies. In fact, Karen and I were leaving Doug, now two years old, home with a professional babysitter for the first time. As we flew from Dallas to Miami on a cold February day, I decided I should call Karly before we boarded the ship and went incommunicado for four days. I wasn't able to get to a phone until we had checked our baggage and were about to go up the gangplank. I called Karly, who told me Campbell had offered me the job of media manager at thirty-five thousand dollars per year, with a few other minor perks.

I was elated and apprehensive at the same time. It would be the career move I was seeking, but not for the money I had hoped for. There would be no negotiation on the salary, according to Karly, as Campbell had strict pay scales for every job. They would, however, pay for a house-hunting trip and pick up all moving expenses. It was the job I'd been seeking, and I told Karly that I was 90 percent sure I'd take it, but asked if I could have four days to make a final decision. She said yes, so Karen and I set sail with a big decision to make. I felt badly about going on a cruise with my T-L colleagues, fairly sure that I would be resigning once we returned to Dallas, but I couldn't resign then. Our berths were booked on the *Flavia*, and I was scheduled to take part in T-L's presentation of the upcoming advertising campaign to the Pizza Inn franchisees. So we scrambled on board with everybody else, and prepared to have a good time and do some thinking.

The cruise on the *Flavia* was great. Even though it was an older ship, it was still a luxury liner, with all that went with it. Pizza Inn had rented the entire ship, so everyone on board was a comrade, mostly franchisees and their wives. All expenses were paid, including our bar tabs. The only exception was the casino, where everyone was on his own. It gave us a chance to mingle with the Pizza Inn franchisees, as well as the company's managers. They liked to have a good time, which made things enjoyable, but we also attended seminars, panel discussions, and speeches from fast-food industry experts.

One evening we were addressed by an editor from *Nation's Restaurant News*, one of the premier trade publications in its field. The speaker relayed some good information about the fast-food industry in general, and pizza in particular. He had a very strong New York accent, and we all took note of the way he said "pizza." As any New Yawka knows, it's pronounced "peetser," which the predominantly Midwestern and Southern franchisee group found terribly amusing.

Our advertising campaign—new research, creative approach, and media plans—were successfully presented to the franchisee group. We had our work cut out for us, as Pizza Hut had over ten times the media budget that Pizza Inn was able to spend. The creative used an Indian swami to declare the pizza "excellent." The media plan called for the use of regional network TV, including some of the high-rated primetime shows at the time: *Mork & Mindy, Taxi, Love Boat, Charlie's Angels*.

The keynote speaker for the entire convention was Ruth

Handler, inventor of the Barbie Doll. She told us how she conceived (not literally) Barbie, based on a German doll, and got the patent on her in 1958. She named the doll after her daughter, Barbara. (Ken, who came later, was named after her son.) When Mattel first presented Barbie at New York's Toyfair in 1959, the toy buyers were very unenthusiastic. But Barbie made it onto a few shelves that year, and by 1960 she was on backorder. Within ten years Barbie and her outfits were selling over five hundred million dollars annually. Ms. Handler's message was a common one in business: if you believe in something you've created, don't let the "experts" discourage you from pushing ahead.

We had a "free" day at Nassau, where we did the usual tourist things—shopping for trinkets, sightseeing, and lying on the beach. There's something about lying on a beautiful beach with a tropical drink, brought to you by a waiter whose goal in life seems to be talking you into another, that says things couldn't be much better, and you should have no concerns. But Karen and I did have a big decision to make, and concerns about the consequences of that decision. Once Campbell's offer was made, we were both inclined to take it, but we still wanted to make sure it was right for us. We both liked Dallas and T-L, had good friends there, and had a house that we enjoyed. On the other hand, it would be a good career move for me, as it met all the criteria I had earlier established for making a change. Doug was two, and would hardly realize a move was taking place, as long as he had his favorite food, Cheerios, and his blanket.

While some of our best friends from T-L were also on the cruise, we didn't seek their counsel about Campbell because it wouldn't have been fair to bring them into the decision at an important time of entertaining and presenting to clients. And I knew what their reactions would be: don't do it. Larry Spelling, my boss, Jo Carlin, a fellow worker, and Kim Kohler, who worked for me, were all on the cruise, and later said I should reconsider leaving T-L. By the end of the cruise we had decided to accept Campbell's offer and move back north.

Upon our return to Dallas I called Karly to confirm the details of the offer from Campbell's, then formally accepted it. I stipulated that I wanted to leave T-L in a professional manner, and that I would provide as much notice as they reasonably needed. Campbell agreed to that, as I was sure they would.

The first morning back at the office, I reluctantly walked into Larry's office and handed him a short, polite letter of resignation. He was surprised, disappointed, but somewhat understanding. He didn't like his people leaving him, and in some cases took it personally. I explained that I wanted to go to the client side of the business, and that my decision was definitely not due to any dissatisfaction during my four years at T-L. He believed me, and didn't ostracize me. He also appreciated my offer to stick around for an extended period, if needed. Larry knew Bob Bolte, having had him as a client once in New York, and said he was a tough client, very demanding.

After he told upper management that I was leaving, Larry put out an agency-wide memo, a T-L tradition when a senior person resigned from the agency. It was entitled, "A Death in the Family," and said some nice things about me, which made me feel very good. Another tradition when somebody left was to have their going-away party at Lombardi's, a terrific Italian restaurant that we frequented as often as possible. For senior people, it was a dinner with spouses, preceded by an appropriately long cocktail "hour." Dinner was followed by speeches, some roasting and some complimentary remarks. Not only were T-L people invited, but so were some clients and friends in the business. Included that night was Roger Tremblay, my long-time tennis opponent and manager of the *Southern Living* office, as well as other media reps deemed friends of the agency and me.

One attendee was Don Tardiff, a veteran representative of *U.S. News & World Report*. Dan was a real pro who'd had a successful career, and was getting ready to retire in another year or two. When it was his turn to speak, he was short and to the point. He said, "Chris, you didn't often buy me, but you always gave me a hearing and explained your decision to me." That was enough to make the evening for me.

During this time I was trying to make sure that I passed the ball to the appropriate people. Kim Kohler was promoted, and Larry made some other changes in the department's structure. It was decided that three weeks was adequate time for me to stay, meaning I'd start at Campbell the first week in March. I got an official letter from Campbell, stating the terms of my employment, start date, etc. It was very formal compared to the way most agencies did things, but typical of big companies as I was to find out.

I also received a package of instructions for moving. I was to get three competing bids, submit them to Campbell's transportation department, then sit back and let them handle everything. They soon informed me that Mayflower would be moving us, and to expect a call to make arrangements. Mayflower called soon thereafter, and handled our move flawlessly.

At this time we put our house up for sale "by owner." We were lucky, in that Dallas was booming at the time. The housing market was strengthened by the fact that American Airlines was in the process of moving its corporate headquarters to the "Metroplex," as Dallas/Ft. Worth had come to be called. In two weeks we had sold it ourselves, at the full asking price. Sales of houses in Texas are handled in a very informal manner. As the sellers, Karen and I went into the mortgage company's office in the morning, and with no lawyers present, signed the sales papers and left the keys. We left the keys and walked out with our check. The buyers came in that afternoon, signed their papers, paid their costs, and walked out with the keys. Ever since then, I've wondered why things can't be handled as simply in other states, but that's just another way in which Texas is different. For that reason, and many others, we knew we'd miss it.

Karen and I took a weekend in February to go to the Philadelphia/Camden area to look for a house. A few of my fraternity brothers lived in the area, so we got lots of good advice as to where to buy. We soon decided to live in southern New Jersey, so I could avoid going across either the Walt Whitman or Ben Franklin Bridge every day. After two days of looking we ended up buying the first house our real estate agent had shown us, a Dutch colonial in Haddonfield,

New Jersey. Haddonfield was an old colonial town about twenty minutes away from Campbell Plaza. We had a blast on the trip, getting reacquainted with a few long-lost Phi Delta Theta brothers one evening. It was nice having a ready-made circle of friends as we made the long move.

Soon after our return to Dallas the movers came and packed everything. We said our last goodbyes to friends and coworkers, had one more great meal in Dallas, then boarded a plane to the Philadelphia airport. We brought Doug and our cat along, picked up a rental car—ours were in the van—and headed to the Sheraton Hotel on Route 70, where we'd stay for a while until we closed on the house.

The night before I started at Campbell, we got together with Tom and Marianne Gorrell, Doug's godparents. They lived in nearby Lindenwold, New Jersey, and I was godfather to their son, Scott. Despite the temptation to stay out late, we had the two young boys with us, so we ended the evening early. As we prepared for bed, Doug began crying. He had a crib in our room, so we turned off all the lights, except for the TV, and hoped for the best. Unfortunately, Doug kept crying with what later turned out to be an ear infection. Finally, about two in the morning, Karen took him down to the hotel lobby so I could get some sleep. I finally drifted off about three, awoke around six, and got ready to report to Campbell's G.O. at eight.

After a quick breakfast, Karen and Doug drove me to Campbell Plaza. We drove through Camden, a decaying city with high unemployment, crime problems, and a corrupt government. The city had definitely seen better days, and was continuing its downward spiral. I would learn later that there were two rival motorcycle gangs that blatantly violated the law, as they battled each other for turf and everything that went with it. The two gangs were named "The Ghetto Riders" and "The Wheels of Soul." They fought constantly, killed each other once in a while, and observed a day's truce every Thanksgiving. On that day they would gather illegally on a street in Camden, close it down, and roast a few pigs. Nobody tried to stop them.

Amidst all this blight was Campbell Plaza, a campus consisting of the two-story main building, several smaller buildings, a parking garage for top executives and a huge parking lot for the rest of us. Off to the side of the main building was the Campbell Museum, which housed an expensive display of soup tureens and other soup paraphernalia. There were sidewalks and lawns with beautiful grass that made this oasis stand out even more from the rest of Camden. Campbell's original soup plant was several blocks away. While still in operation, it was very small and inefficient compared to the new ones scattered around the country.

I arrived half an hour before the official opening at eight in the morning, and met Bob Bolte in the lobby. The lobby was large, decorated very simply with cans and packages of all the Campbell products, and had a soup tureen, from which visitors could help themselves as they waited. Bob introduced me to Lorraine, the receptionist. Lorraine was the dictator of the reception area, with a loud voice and hearty laugh. She reminded me of Miss Kittie on the old *Gunsmoke* series. Like Dottie "Lobby" at Y&R, Lorraine remembered every visitor's name and would greet them with a comment about their clothes or business. I later found out she had been in the theater, as a dancer. I grew to like her, though she seemed out of place at a conservative company such as Campbell's Soup.

Bob welcomed me, and we headed upstairs to get a cup of coffee in the huge cafeteria, which offered soup every day for ten cents a bowl. References to soup, and pictures of the Campbell Kids were everywhere. That, and the fact that the word "soup" was still in the company's name, pointed up the dominance of soup to the company, despite its dozens of other products,

Shortly after I started at Campbell I began to realize how much a part of Americana the company had become. Besides residing in almost every home in the country, its Red & White soup cans were recognized around the world as an American icon. And that wasn't just Campbell propaganda. The fact is that Andy Warhol, on his own, chose to paint the Campbell Soup can as his idea of an American symbol, along with other icons such as Marilyn Monroe.

His first soup-can painting was done in 1962. At first the company didn't like being associated with such a "radical." But as times changed, so did Campbell's attitude. In 1985, as part of its effort to get into the dry soup market, Campbell introduced Campbell's dry soup mix, with the packets of dehydrated soup coming in a Red & White box. Guess who Campbell **paid** to paint the "Campbell Box"? None other than Andy Warhol, whom they also hired to attend a few press parties and other events. Unfortunately, Campbell's dry soup wasn't the success they hoped for. But the fact that they hired Andy Warhol showed how much the country and the company had changed from the midsixties to the mideighties.

CHAPTER ELEVEN

Firing Miss America

Even though I'd read up on Campbell's as part of the interviewing process and preparing for arrival, Bob plied me with additional information that morning. And as I picked up additional details during my time at the company, I developed an appreciation for how big and diverse Campbell's was. I saw this as well its quirks.

Campbell had annual sales that year of two billion dollars. Its thirty-four thousand employees worked around the world, producing over five hundred different products. Approximately 88 percent of its sales were in the U.S., with soup accounting for the greatest percentage of sales volume and profit. The company is publicly traded on the NYSE, and is controlled by the Dorrance family of Philadelphia. They are descendants of John T. Dorrance, who invented condensed soup in 1897 while working for the Joseph Campbell Preserve Company. The Dorrance family collectively owns about one-third of the company's stock, and heavily influences another one-third through trusts. At the time, Jack Dorrance was chairman of the board. He has since passed away, but the family still dominates the board, and no CEO is named without their approval.

Campbell's had started in Philadelphia in 1869 as a produce canner, known for its oversize beefsteak tomatoes. Its condensed soups sold well, as the country's population shifted from farms to cities. Throughout its history, advertising has played a big role in its success. Just a few years after introducing canned soup, Campbell bought ad space on a few streetcars in New York City. A year later, sales were up so much that it bought ads on **every** streetcar in New

York. Today, Campbell's Soup is one of the biggest sellers of any product in supermarkets, and the average home has seven cans of Red & White Soup in its cupboard at any given time.

While in business to make money, the company is benevolent in the way it treats its customers, employees, and even suppliers. As it was explained to me early on, if a farmer is having trouble growing peas that aren't good enough for Campbell, the company will send one of its agronomists to help with the problem, at no charge to the farmer. Campbell has always worked hard to develop and enhance its image as a benign, family-oriented company. The Campbell Kids, "born" in 1904, were just part of the effort to project that image. Its advertising was always wholesome, and it sponsored upstanding programs such as the *Campbell Playhouse* on radio and *Lassie* on television. It also used popular celebrities to endorse its products, including Ronald Reagan for V8 in the fifties. To this day it still uses celebrities and athletes—with "clean" reputations—to promote its products.

Campbell's image took a big hit in the midseventies, at least within the advertising community. BBD&O was filming a commercial for Red & White Soup, and wanted to show how thick and full of garnish the soup was. (As everyone at Campbell quickly learns, there are two parts to soup: the broth, or liquid part, and the garnish, which is meat, vegetables, or other solid matter within the broth.) Before the filming, someone put marbles in the bottom of the soup bowl, to make sure the garnish was more visible to the camera.

This "trick" was leaked to the press, causing much embarrassment to both Campbell and BBD&O. Of course, Campbell got most of the bad press, which many people, including the media, seemed to relish in light of the company's otherwise squeaky-clean reputation. Campbell was so distraught at the bad publicity that it instituted a new policy for commercial production. It became mandatory that a member of the company's in-house kitchen/homemaking staff be present on the set of every commercial shoot. Their main job was to make sure that the company and its agencies didn't become "overzealous" again.

Years later, Campbell learned that it was another food company, Heinz, that had blown the whistle on the "marble" ad. This was in retribution for Campbell's overpowering counterattack a few years beforehand, when Heinz had introduced its "Great American Soup" line. Heinz had the audacity to challenge Campbell with a full frontal assault on its main line of Red & White condensed soups. That was Pearl Harbor and the sinking of the *Maine* all in one. When Heinz did that, Campbell pulled out all the stops to kill the Great American brand, and succeeded. This perpetuated the "bad blood" that had existed between the two Pennsylvania companies for decades. A few years later it was rumored that Campbell retaliated for the marble incident by tipping off the SEC that Heinz was juggling its books to make quarterly earnings look better. The wars go on.

The main soup line was "Red & White," which referred to the regular line of soups that we all think of when someone says Campbell's, in the familiar 10.75 ounce cans. Chunky was the leading ready-to-eat soup, and Soup-for-One was a small line, made for seniors or other people wanting a single portion from one can. Speaking of cans, Campbell manufactured its own cans, and was the second-largest can maker in the country.

Other Campbell brands include Swanson, Pepperidge Farm, V8, Vlasic Pickles, Franco-American pasta products, Recipe dog food, and Godiva chocolates. During the time I was there, Campbell purchased Mrs. Paul's, and successfully launched Prego spaghetti sauce. The company was also in the restaurant business, operating Pietro's, a West Coast pizza chain, and Hanover Trails, a chain of steak houses in the East.

Campbell used the brand manager system, which made each brand and division its own profit center. Our group within the Marketing Department was called Advertising Services, and as such we interacted with all the brand managers. Our mission was to provide media and promotional support to the brands; help select, compensate, and review advertising agencies; and act as the liaison between the brand managers and the media departments of the agencies. Our unwritten mission, along with the entire Marketing

Department, was to protect the Red & White Soup line's 75 percent share of market, and grow the other Campbell brand's into the leading product in their categories. As was often said in strategy meetings, "The scenery only changes for the lead dog."

We employed several of the top agencies in the country. BBD&O handled the Red & White soups, as well as Chunky. Ogilvy & Mather was our agency for Pepperidge Farm and Swanson Frozen foods. Godiva was at Margeotes/Fertitta & Partners. Swanson soups and gravies, Franco-American, as well as V8, were handled by Needham, Harper & Steers in Chicago. Vlasic pickles were served by W.B. Doner in Detroit. We had a few smaller agencies for grocery trade efforts, military advertising, the restaurant chains, and some of the smaller brands. For some other minor assignments, we also had an in-house agency, CSC Advertising, which was staffed by people like me, used on an ad hoc basis.

We were a big-name advertiser, spent big bucks, and were highly demanding of our agencies. As such, we got the top talent from most of them on our business. Campbell brands were known to be tough ones to work on at agencies. When someone was assigned to a Campbell brand at BBD&O they got this speech:

"You're going to work on a great brand, and you'll learn the Campbell way. You'll hate it at first, but you'll see how a top brand is kept on top. Give them your professional opinion, but remember they've got a 75 percent share of the canned soup market, and they know what they're doing. Give it your all, and if you don't like it after a year, we'll reassign you to another client."

If they were in the media department at an agency, one of us would typically call them and welcome them to the Campbell's business. We echoed what their agency bosses had warned them about, saying that it wouldn't be as bad as they had described—it would be worse. But we also promised them that they'd learn a lot, and we expected 110 percent from them for a year, or however long they were on our account. Many of them then asked the same question: which airport did they fly into when they came for meetings, Philadelphia? We were always amused by this question, and advised them that all they had to do was drive about ninety miles down the Jersey Turnpike, or take Amtrak to Philadelphia, then a cab (make sure you get the special Campbell rate) across the bridge to Camden.

The weaker, less-dedicated people did leave the account after a year or so. But the good ones, wanting a challenge, stayed on for years, and became an ingredient in Campbell's successes. Campbell's agencies were integral to the success of its brands for many reasons. One was the fact that we relied on our agencies to do a lot of the heavy lifting, as we directed them from Camden. Campbell ran lean and mean. I saw an example of this shortly after I arrived. The Red & White brand group consisted of four people, overseeing the line with about nine hundred million dollars in sales. When one of the four left, another assistant brand manager was hired from Revlon and brought down from New York. At his first meeting with the other three brand managers, he looked around, and asked, "Where's everybody else?" "What do you mean," asked Paul Mulcahy, the brand director. The new recruit replied, "At Revlon, my brand did $140 million in sales, and we had six brand managers." Paul explained that soup didn't have the same margins as cosmetics, and wasn't able to support such a hierarchy. The guy from Revlon quit in less than a week after his arrival.

Several of us in the Marketing Department, especially those in Advertising Services, had worked at advertising agencies prior to joining Campbell. Life at Campbell was highly regimented compared to the much-looser style at agencies. Whereas agencies tended to be loose and casual, Campbell was tight and formal. Everyone at the G.O. was expected to be in at 8:00, when we started work. There was no bell, as in a high school, but attendance was taken each morning by the department head's secretary. Though we were salaried employees, we were regimented as if we were hourly employees at the plants. As in the plants, no men were allowed to have facial hair. But at least we didn't have to wear the hair nets that the plant workers did. There was no eating at your desk. Once each morning and afternoon there was a fifteen-minute break, when you could walk around or go to the cafeteria for coffee.

Smoking was not permitted in the buildings, but you could

go outside and stand around with one of the many groups who socialized while smoking, no matter the weather. The funny thing was that after five, smoking was permitted inside the buildings. If a meeting went past five o'clock, the smokers would pull out their smokes and ashtrays, and light up in the middle of the meeting. This was a variance from the policy in the plants, as there was no smoking in them at any time.

There were shoe shine kits in each men's room, which were kept immaculate. Men were expected to keep their shoes properly shined at all times. And if a man left his department's area, he was supposed to put on his suit jacket. If you wore a sports jacket or a short-sleeved shirt to work, it meant that you didn't care about getting promoted. Lunch was an hour, either to be spent in the cafeteria, or if you were fast enough, you could make it to a nearby restaurant. That typically meant getting in a car and driving to a safer area than the one immediately surrounding Campbell Plaza.

Those of us who had worked elsewhere, and particularly ad agencies, found these rules highly confining, and we disregarded several of them. We weren't as blatant about it as the characters on *M.A.S.H.*, but we flouted these restrictions, and got away with it. We did follow the "suit and no short-sleeve shirt" rule, however, as we wanted to be promoted. The other Campbell employees regarded us as mavericks, or even rebels. They were amazed that we'd stay out "late" for lunch, or wouldn't take every fifteen-minute break available to us.

We got away with it primarily for one reason—we worked later and longer than any other department. At five o'clock the stampede out the door would start, as virtually every employee headed home when the whistle—figuratively—blew. But those of us in Advertising Services, and many in the rest of the Marketing Department, didn't leave with the crowd. While casual in many ways, we also maintained our prior work habits, prevalent in service businesses: we worked until the job was done. While most work areas and hallways were deserted after five o'clock, the Marketing Department was still working. That was the unofficial covenant that kept the discipline police off our backs.

Someone reading this might think that Campbell was a controlling, stifling company, and in some ways it was. But it was also very benevolent, in that it took care of its people. For example, there were two full-time dentists on staff, meaning if you came in one morning with a cavity, you could have it taken care of that afternoon. And it would only cost you ten dollars. Every potential employee was given a physical exam before being hired, at no charge. If anything wrong was found, Campbell would have it treated, again at no charge, once you became an employee. I came in with a bad case of tendinitis in my shoulder, from playing too much tennis. There was a complete "minihospital" inside the G.O., staffed by two M.D.'s. The mandatory physical confirmed the tendinitis. I was given ultrasound treatments three times a week for several months until it cleared up, then charged the usual rate—nothing.

Sometimes the formalities of the bureaucracy became laughable. At one point, Herb Baum was promoted from Director of New Products to VP Marketing. Being a vice president of the company meant that he was entitled to carpeting in his office. But his office in the Marketing Department area had a linoleum floor, as they all did. It took several weeks before Herb moved to the long corridor in the main building where the company VP's officed. Shortly after his promotion was announced, some workers appeared in his large corner office, and covered his linoleum floor with beautiful carpeting. That'll be terrific for the next person who moves into that office, I thought. Within days after Herb moved to his new office on VP row, the same workers appeared at his old office again, and ripped up the five-week-old carpet. Under Campbell's rules, only VP's got carpets in their offices, no matter how nice it would have been for the next person. I know rank has its privileges, but I could never understand that kind of bureaucratic waste.

One of our assignments in Advertising Services was to act as guardians of the Campbell public image. The company was very protective of its proprietary property—patents, copyrights, etc.— as well as its reputation as a "clean" company, dedicated to providing wholesome products to the American public at a fair price. That reputation had been built up over the years in many ways, including its use of radio and television commercials. During radio's "Golden Age," Campbell sponsored *The Campbell Playhouse*, which put on high-class shows. One that is still played on a few stations around the holidays is a version of Dickens' *A Christmas Carol*, starring Lionel Barrymore as Scrooge.

Campbell's sponsorship of the program resulted from a famous incident in 1938. Orson Welles and his *Mercury Theatre on the Air* performed its famous *War of the Worlds* that year, scaring most of the country as it reported the Martian landings in New Jersey. Welles and his cast—which included John Houseman, who would later become quite a spokesman himself—became overnight sensations, and Campbell jumped in as the sole sponsor of the *Mercury Theatre* in 1939, and changed the name to *The Campbell Playhouse* in 1940.

In the early days of television, Campbell had sponsored *Lassie*, one of the most wholesome TV shows ever, as well as *The Donna Reed Show*, a real family program. One of our duties was to make sure our agencies continued that tradition, and purchased commercials only in television programs that had no gratuitous sex or violence. There was a detailed policy statement that outlined Campbell's policies in specific terms. We also maintained an ongoing list of shows that were to be avoided. The list was long, and even included *All in the Family*, because of some of the topics the show addressed. While comparatively mild now, much of the language was "cutting edge" at the time.

Also, at this time, Reverend Wildmon, the Mississippi guardian of America's morals, was keeping watch on which companies were advertising on objectionable (to him) programs. Campbell wanted to avoid being listed by Reverend Wildmon or anyone else as a company that advertised on the "wrong" shows. Just as bad was getting even a few letters from people complaining about where they saw our ads. Company policy dictated that each one was to receive an answering letter, explaining our policy. Sometimes the letters included an apology if, by mistake, a Campbell ad had run in a program on the banned list. In addition to providing our "no-

no list," our instructions to the agencies who bought TV time for us was, "When in doubt, leave it out."

Campbell's agencies, like most major agencies, employed a screening service in New York. This service viewed all upcoming network TV programs, looking for potential trouble spots, and alerting the agencies (and us at Campbell's through them) to potentially undesirable scenes. If an upcoming program contained objectionable material, we'd be warned about it, and we could pull out of the episode entirely, or simply ask the network to move our ad to another, less-controversial, part of the program. The service would also protect us from inappropriate placement of our ads. For example, if we advertised in *M.A.S.H.* we didn't want an ad for tomato soup to appear right after a scene in which Hawkeye had finished operating, and was wearing scrubs with "blood" all over them.

We especially liked programming in which the content was wholesome, predictable, and to some degree, controlled by the company. Few of these existed, but when they did, Campbell tried to participate. The Miss America Pageant in Atlantic City was one of those opportunities. It was perfect for Campbell's advertising, and the company was a longtime sponsor of the event, along with Kellogg's and Gillette. What could be a better program? The show always got a good rating, had a heavily female audience, and the content was as pure and wholesome as the fifty contestants. This was before some of the later controversies had occurred. And to top it all off, Atlantic City was only an hour away from Camden, meaning we could go to the final event, always televised on a Saturday night. In fact, BBD&O usually had a nice cocktail party and dinner for its participating clients, Campbell and Gillette. And, as sponsors, we could go into the NBC production trailer and watch the show from behind the scenes. We could also watch the press conference, which was not televised, after the new Miss America was crowned.

Everything about the Miss America Pageant was perfect for Campbell. Perfect until one day when the president, Harold Shaub, an engineer by trade, proclaimed the pageant as too expensive. In marketing, we were incredulous, as we were even using Lee Meriwether, a former Miss America, as our spokeswoman. For a long time she had endorsed the Light Ones, a group of Red & White soups with fewer than ninety calories per serving.

Mr. Shaub contended that the cost of sponsoring the pageant had grown too expensive. On a cost-per-thousand basis it was somewhat more expensive than ordinary programs, but that's typical of most high-rated programs. But his main concern was that the pageant committee had suddenly fired longtime master of ceremonies, Bert Parks. Mr. Parks had been the voice and host of the pageant for many years, but had committed the cardinal sin of television: he had grown old. His firing was done awkwardly, without warning and with very little grace, and the pageant got a black eye in the media from the manner in which it was handled.

Of course, we in the Marketing Department recognized the unfortunate handling of Mr. Parks' firing, but we felt the bad press wouldn't detract from the pageant's ratings or the reputations of the sponsors. We believed people recognized that the sponsors didn't have control over who served as host. After much discussion, Mr. Shaub reluctantly agreed to continue with the sponsorship, but his attitude was, "nothing else better go wrong with this thing." While jubilant over our victory, we worried about another "incident."

That "incident" occurred at the very next pageant in 1980. Several of us traveled to Atlantic City to attend BBD&O's party, and to see the event. At the cocktail party I ran into Tom Ryan, who had been a member of Waccabuc Country Club when I worked there. He was now one of the top advertising executives at Gillette. I remembered serving him at Waccabuc, and I walked up to him and introduced myself. He sort of remembered me after more than ten years. For some reason I remembered that Early Times and soda was his drink, and asked him if that was what he was drinking that night. He was surprised that I remembered, and we had a nice talk about advertising in general and the pageant itself. Tom said it was the perfect program for several Gillette personal care products.

The pageant went off perfectly, with Miss Louisiana being named Miss America. Like all the contestants, she was talented and pretty. We all agreed it would be fun when she visited Campbell Plaza in a few days, which was included in the sponsorship package. The press conference started about one in the morning, with the usual questions, and the new Miss America handling herself well. Karen and I watched it, then drove back to Haddonfield to sleep late.

In a few days, Miss America came to visit Campbell's Soup, walked around awhile, had lunch, and left. A few days after that, the storm erupted. While not widely reported before the pageant, the media later carried a story about Miss America. She maintained that she had been in a bad motorcycle accident a few years earlier. She had an operation on her leg to repair her injuries, causing it to become six inches shorter than her other leg. She then expanded on the story, saying that through prayer, she had caused the short leg to grow by six inches, so it again matched the length of her other leg. Miss America was born again. Her announcement was met with a lot of skepticism, and some controversy. That was it for Mr. Shaub. The day after the story hit word came down to us from his office that Campbell would definitely **not** renew its sponsorship of the Miss America Pageant. There were no volunteers to argue with him this time.

In January of 1981 we added another member to our family. Karen had been pregnant for the usual nine months, and we had expected our second child before Christmas, but nothing happened. One cold Saturday night in January we had a few people over for dinner, including Ted Field, the brand manager on Chunky. Ted and his wife Nancy lived nearby in Cherry Hills, and we had become good friends. As we began dinner, Karen said it was time to go to the hospital. The little party broke up, Doug went home with the Fields, and I took Karen across the Walt Whitman Bridge to Pennsylvania Hospital, which had been founded by Ben Franklin.

About five o'clock the next morning our second son, Andrew, was born with me watching. Everything went according to plan, and we brought Andrew home in a few days. Karen and I had a laugh on the way home as I told her about an article I had read that day in *The Wall St. Journal*. Some professor had done a study measuring the stability of marriages based on the combination of kids in those marriages. He had found that married couples with two boys stayed together more than couples with any other combination of kids. He surmised that this was because two boys were such a handful that they drove their parents into an alliance to meet the challenges they faced. We were soon testing his theory.

And speaking of tests, we were conducting a very significant test at the time for Campbell's Red & White soups. It involved repositioning the entire line, and resulted from extensive testing with consumers and documentation with health boards and government agencies. The campaign's theme was "Soup Is Good Food," and positioned soup as being healthy and nutritious, as well as tasting good. Nobody felt the need to put "Campbell's" in the headline, as we owned the category with a 75 percent share of market. The campaign was developed by Jim Backer, while he was at McCann-Erickson. It was about to be tested when Backer and Carl Spielvogel broke away from McCann and formed Backer & Spielvogel. They started out with a nice little piece of business called Miller Lite, which they had worked on at McCann. The brand had a budget of about eighty million dollars, most of it in network sports programming, and Miller Lite was thought to be the most profitable account in the business. Whether it was or not, everyone who worked on it had a lot of fun making the "tastes great, less filling" commercials with the sports celebrities.

Jim Backer had helped conceive the "Soup Is Good Food" campaign, and had overseen its development at McCann-Erickson. Despite Campbell's loyalty to its agencies, upper management was watching this campaign evolve, and decided it was too important to leave at McCann without Backer. So the "Soup Is Good Food" campaign was awarded to B&S, with the stipulation that Jim Backer would continue to be heavily involved in it. BBD&O kept the main portion of Red & White Soup advertising.

Once the campaign was ready to run, it was decided to test it on the West Coast, for two reasons. One was that people on the West Coast are known to be more health-conscious than the rest of the country, and we wanted to see if it generated results with them. The second reason was that we could easily place the test copy on the networks' West Coast feeds, while continuing the regular campaign ("It's Right on Your Shelf") in the rest of the country. We could essentially do the same thing with national magazines, as well as buy West Coast publications such as *Sunset* and *Los Angeles.*

The West Coast network feeds and the West Coast editions of magazines encompassed the Pacific time zone, about 15 percent of the U.S. population. This was bigger than typical test-market areas, but we wanted a truly reliable, projectable reading. The TV ran in the usual array of tasteful programs acceptable to Campbell's strict guidelines—daytime soaps and selected primetime shows. But in magazines we adopted a new strategy. The "Soup Is Good Food" statement was treated as "news," so we ran ads in the newsweeklies instead of the usual women's service magazines. A food ad in *Time* and *Newsweek* really stood out, causing readers, we believed, to sit up and think, "What's this doing here?" and hyping the ad's readership.

Something worked, as sales rose 3 percent in the test area compared to the rest of the country. This may not seem like a big increase, but it was significant for Campbell. We were fighting lifestyle and demographic trends that made canned soup a slow-growth category. As we said, every time someone moves from Detroit to Dallas they eat one less can of soup a year, purely from the temperature change. So even 3 percent growth on fifty-five million cases a year meant a lot more soup being consumed.

"The Soup is Good Food" campaign was deemed a complete success, and was rolled out nationally. It was B&S's work that had done it, and eventually they were rewarded. After twenty-six years at BBD&O the Red & White soup business account was switched to B&S. BBD&O kept Chunky and Soup-for-One. It was a big move that brought another major agency into Campbell's tent.

Campbell often used upstanding celebrities in its advertising, especially if they were somehow appropriate for the brand using them. One such case was getting Tommy Lasorda and Steve Garvey to endorse Swanson's Hungry-Man frozen dinners. Hungry-Man was made for hearty eaters, and contained two man-sized helpings of the main dish—two chicken breasts, two Swiss steaks, etc. At the time, Tommy Lasorda's Dodgers were big winners, due in part to the stellar play of Steve Garvey. Even better, Lasorda was known as a hearty eater, who often talked about how much pasta he consumed, and he had the body to prove it.

This was perfect for Hungry-Man. Swanson and Ogilvy & Mather filmed a commercial with Tommy and Steve in their uniforms, eating Hungry-Man dinners in the dugout. As in most food commercials where the actors eat—or pretend to eat—the product, there was a large "spit-bucket" just off-camera for them to spit the food into after each take. Most commercials require many, many takes to get it right, and when actors have to do take after take, they usually can't eat every bite the cameras record. John Haring, the Hungry-Man brand manager, was telling us about meeting the two celebrities out in L.A., where the spot was filmed. Since both were heroes to many of us, John had a rapt audience. One guy asked him if Lasorda had really liked the Hungry-Man chicken. "He must have," answered John, "I never saw him use the spit-bucket once." To illustrate how much peoples' images can change, remember this: about ten years later, Tommy Lasorda was doing commercials for Slim-Fast.

One day the craziness of how the media business works was brought home to me—by some accountants. A team from Campbell's accounting firm showed up for an audit of the marketing department. Two young men asked for a couple hours of my time, and got it—I never argue with accountants. They had been through our records for buying media over the last few quarters. Actually, our agencies had bought it for us, at our direction. One of the young men pulled out a network TV schedule for Pepperidge Farm cookies, totaling just over two million dollars for the current quarter. It was currently running on all three broadcast networks, as well as Superstation TBS. "How does something like this get authorized?" one asked.

"The brand manager here signs the proposed schedule, and we give the agency our approval to buy it," I answered.

"Yes, I know how it works internally at Campbell," the accountant continued, "I'm interested in how it works between Campbell, the agency, and the networks."

"We give the agency our approval, then they place the order with each network," I replied.

"What about paperwork, signed approvals?" Mr. Accountant asked.

"Between us and the agency?"

"Yes, and between the agency and the networks."

"There is no paperwork until the computers print it up and send it out, usually after the schedule's started, or finished if it's a short one."

He was amazed. "So two million dollars worth of network TV runs without the agency or networks having a signed approval, from Campbell or between themselves?"

"That's right," I responded, "it's all based on trust, with paperwork catching up later. If you're a known network player, you can call up CBS or any other network and order ten million dollars' worth of time, just on your word."

"Jesus Christ," they both said. "What if you're not really authorized to spend the money, or what if someone is ordering, then not intending to pay?"

"I said **known** player. You have to be in the club, or you can't do it. And if you ever go back on your word, you're out of the club forever, and word spreads fast."

The two accountants were now taking notes and saying "Hmmmm" to themselves. They couldn't believe it, and when I thought about it, I realized how strange these customs must seem to people who, quite logically, think that there must be mountains of authorizations, purchase orders, and other paperwork before even a small amount of money can be spent. Because network TV moves so fast, and the "club" is so small, it almost has to work that way. There's a high level of trust and professionalism, and anyone who violates that trust is thrown out, and isn't allowed in again.

CHAPTER TWELVE

Blood on My Briefcase

In mid-1981 things were going well at Campbell. Prego Spaghetti Sauce had exceeded goals in test market and was getting ready to roll out nationally. At home, we were getting comfortable with taking care of two boys. A couple of weeks before we were scheduled to spend a week on the Jersey Shore, I came back from lunch, and Pam, my secretary, handed me a stack of phone messages. One call was from a "Mr. Clear" at McCann-Erickson in Atlanta. I didn't know who he was, but McCann in New York had worked on the "Soup Is Good Food" campaign, so I thought it might pertain to that and returned the call. On the other end of the line was a gravelly-voiced gentleman with a thick Southern accent. It belonged to Chuck Clear, and he quickly let me know that he had been given my name by Mike Fitzgerald, a magazine rep who had called on us at Tracy-Locke in Dallas. Mike lived in Atlanta, was a very successful independent publisher's representative, had an engaging personality, and knew practically everyone in the advertising business throughout the South. Mike and I had become good friends over the years, and when he recommended that someone call, I knew it would be something worthwhile.

Chuck was second in command at the McCann-Erickson office in Atlanta. He told me McCann was looking for a media director, and that I should consider coming back to the agency business, and the South. McCann's big account in Atlanta was Coca-Cola, along with several others. And they were getting the Georgia-Pacific account, as G-P was moving to Atlanta from Portland, Oregon. The career opportunity sounded good, and I had missed the agency side of the business, as well as the South. I told him I'd think about it, and call him back within two days.

I talked with Karen about the possibility of moving to Atlanta. She had spent a year there after college, and liked it, describing it as "a lot like Dallas, but with trees." We decided that I would continue talking with Chuck and McCann. After a few more telephone conversations, Chuck invited me to come to Atlanta for a visit and interview. I did some research on McCann and its parent company, Interpublic. This was easy, as several of the people at Backer & Spielvogel had come from McCann in New York. I was also sure that the folks at McCann had checked up on me in a similar manner.

The day came for me to fly to Atlanta. I took an evening flight from Philadelphia, arrived in Atlanta after dinner, and went to bed early at the Colony Square Hotel. The next day I had a quick breakfast and was picked up by Chuck's secretary, Marcy, who explained that Chuck's car was in the shop. It was a 1968 Mercedes SL that I would find later was in the shop on a regular basis, as Chuck was constantly "restoring" it. We arrived at the McCann offices on North Avenue and Peachtree Street, within sight of the massive Coke Tower.

Marcy took me to Elliot Abernathy's large corner office on the sixth floor of the building, and introduced us. Elliot was McCann's general manager in Atlanta, the youngest in the McCann system. He was a Georgia boy who had gone to Wharton for his MBA, started his career at JWT in Chicago, and risen through the ranks in account service. We had a good discussion about the Atlanta office, and what he thought was needed in the Media Department. He had read my resume, and thought I had the experience needed for the job. After a while Chuck Clear came into the office, and we all talked about the job. Chuck and Elliot had grown up together in the same small town in southern Georgia. Both had gone to the University of Georgia and were rabid Bulldog fans. They had a good relationship, and their wives were also good friends.

Chuck brought me around to meet and talk with some other senior people at the agency, including Len Farbo, the creative director. We had a good meeting, even though creative directors and media directors aren't known for always getting along. Media people like to keep costs down by using small-space black-and-white ads, while creatives want big spreads with four colors, maybe even five.

After some informal discussions, and a few real interviews, it was time for lunch. After a full morning, I was impressed by the people and the work that McCann was doing. While a lot revolved around Coke, there were several other clients that provided diversity, including Continental Telephone, Six Flags, Lockheed, and an up-and-coming fast-food company called Chick-fil-A.

After a meeting with Jake Roucher, the management supervisor on Chick-fil-A, Chuck and Elliot came by, and the four of us drove downtown to lunch. We headed toward the Capital City Club, a prestigious businessman's club, which also featured a golf course close to the city. While on the way, we hit downtown Atlanta's notorious traffic, and at one point were sitting in it, waiting to move again. Next to us was a large, brightly colored van, shaking and blaring loud music. Three guys were half-sitting, half-dancing on the front seat, paying little attention to traffic. We all looked over at it, and after a minute Elliot asked no one in particular, "What do you think has gone on in that van?" Without missing a beat, Chuck answered back, "What do you think **hasn't** gone on in that van?" It was at that point that I decided these would be fun people to work with. The "fun factor" is often overlooked by people when they're deciding on a job. To me, it was as important as the title, the actual work, and the salary.

We had a nice lunch, then headed back to McCann's offices. I interviewed with some more people and met a few of the members of the Media Department. It seemed a little strange to be meeting people you **might** lead later, but when in Rome . . . I caught a plane to Philadelphia about six, and made my way back to the Jersey Shore at a very late hour.

The next day I learned that my father had had his leg amputated, as a result of cancer. For six months the doctors at Columbia-Presbyterian in New York had been trying to save it, but hadn't been able to do so. It was a shock, of course, but the long-term prognosis seemed good. Elliot called a few days later and offered me the position of vice president, media director of McCann's Atlanta office. While I wanted to accept, Karen and I agreed that I would decline because of the uncertain status of my father. In hindsight, it seems ridiculous, but I worried about who would mow my parents' lawn in Katonah if we weren't three hours away. After my brothers and I left home, my father had mowed it, but I didn't think he'd be able to do it with one leg. That, and the related concerns, caused me to turn down Elliot's offer with regret, explaining my concerns to him.

Over the next few days my father's condition and prognosis improved. We left the shore and returned to Haddonfield. I received another call from Elliot, who recognized my situation and offered a potential solution. Added to the previous offer would be ten trips to New York, at McCann's expense, to enable me to help take care of my parents. I was complimented by the offer, and it seemed to be a good solution to my concerns. After discussing it more with Karen, we decided to make the move to Atlanta.

As I expected, leaving Campbell was less of a production than leaving Tracy-Locke. Bob Bolte was disappointed and asked if more money would make me stay. When I told him what McCann was going to pay me he said Campbell couldn't match it. I told him it wasn't all money anyway. We were making the change to go back South and back to the agency side of the business, and that I hoped we'd remain friends. He assured me we would, and, in fact, did come to our house once we were settled in Atlanta. There was a little going-away party for me at a nearby restaurant, an exit interview, and I was gone in two weeks. I knew I'd miss Campbell, but Atlanta in 1981 was an up-and-coming city, and Coca-Cola was a great brand to work on. Plus, I'd be a department head, have VP stripes, and be a member of the executive committee that ran the agency. I was anxious to get started.

We put our house on the market, aggressively priced, and began the moving process. I was to start at McCann in early August, and Karen and the boys would move down in September. We'd have the usual weekend house-hunting trip in the interim, with McCann taking care of all expenses. I got my first indication of how bitter the cola wars were right then. When we received the moving instructions from the Human Relations Department in Atlanta it contained the following directive with regard to choosing a van company: "Obtain three bids for moving all household articles, then select one. You may **not** use the North American Van Lines Company." The reason for this was because Pepsi-Cola owned North American Van Lines. I started to get the picture—it wasn't just a marketing war between Coke and Pepsi, it was an all-out war that extended to all aspects of their businesses and business partners. Pepsi also owned Wilson Sporting Goods at the time. I knew what kind of tennis balls **not** to buy when we got to Atlanta.

I flew to Atlanta on August 1. It's lucky I did, because the air traffic controllers went on strike the next day, causing President Reagan to fire them, resulting in air travel havoc. I checked into the Marriott, about three blocks from McCann's offices at 615 Peachtree Street. It was a decent place, with the best feature being close to Bobby Dodd Stadium at Georgia Tech football, where I could jog after work.

Early on Monday morning I walked to McCann and reported to Elliot Abernathy, McCann's general manager. We had a cup of coffee, and I headed down to the fifth floor to officially meet and take control of the Media Department. I gathered everyone together, made a short speech about making the department the best in the business, keeping lines of communication open, and doing everything possible to give our clients what they needed.

There was quite a cast of characters in the department, the usual hodgepodge of junior people from various backgrounds, led by a cadre of career media professionals. The most senior person was Stan Saltzman, who had moved to Atlanta after a long, undistinguished career in Chicago. He knew the media basics, but had a hard time getting along with people. He didn't keep up on new media trends, such as cable, seeming to ignore its impact on broadcast viewing levels. And he loved to beat up media representatives if they didn't kowtow to his ego and desire for tickets to sporting events. Stan had been passed over for the media director's job, and unsurprisingly, resented my presence. Ours was not to be a happy relationship.

Another peach of a guy was a newly arrived media supervisor. Mitch Stroud had moved to McCann Atlanta from the New York office, reportedly because nobody in New York could stand him. Nobody was sure why they transferred him rather than just firing him. He had no social graces at all, and his former boss allegedly threw pencils and staplers at him. He had a loud, irritating voice that he used constantly. He talked all the time, but rarely said anything intelligent. To watch him eat took away your appetite, and the food he spilled down his shirt mixed with the burn marks from the cigarette ashes that had already soiled it.

One story illustrates Mitch's lack of savoir faire. McCann had pitched a relatively small prospective client a few weeks before I arrived. Following a terrific creative campaign, Mitch had presented the media portion of the speculative advertising campaign, and done a good job. The prospect was impressed and complimented him as the meeting ended. Mitch's response was, "Yeah, but you should see what we can do with a decent budget." Blatantly telling a prospective client that his budget is small is an insult and implies that he won't get full attention from the agency. Unsurprisingly, this prospect selected a competitor to handle his account. Everyone from McCann who had been in the presentation knew why. In a relatively short time, Mitch had alienated half the office—the half that had met him. He saved me from firing him by resigning a few weeks after I arrived. He left the agency business to become a headhunter, of all things.

Then there was Gene Armani, a bright, young media planner on the rise. He had started his career at McCann after graduating from Georgia Tech. Gene worked harder than almost anyone I'd known in the business and was eager to learn more. Clients loved him because he worked so hard on their business and negotiated great media deals for them. He would become an ally and an asset to the department. My main task with Gene was to hold him back from "overnegotiating." One of the media department's jobs is to negotiate favorable rates and positions for its clients. Gene did this, but often took it too far, in that he'd negotiate price with media entities, particularly magazines, to the point where they almost resented getting the business. On the other hand, they could always turn the business down if they didn't like the price.

McCann Atlanta had started as a service office, with the purpose of making sure that it kept close to Coca-Cola. The agency's office was about ten blocks away from the big Coke tower on North Avenue. Between McCann and Coke stood part of Georgia Tech, and a drive-in restaurant called the Varsity. The legend was that the Varsity had been started by a young man who had flunked out of Georgia Tech and decided to show them that he could be a success despite that. The eat-in part of the restaurant was a series of large rooms, all with a TV in the front and college-type desks for the customers to sit in while they watched. The menu consisted mostly of hot dogs, hamburgers, and onion rings that were greasy, but good. Of course, the main drink was Coke. Not only did the Varsity become a huge success, but it grew to be the largest buyer of Coke syrup of any establishment in the world, a distinction it retains to this day.

From its beginning as a service office for Coke, McCann grew to a full-service agency, with several large clients besides Coke. Even so, it was pegged as the "Coke agency" by the advertising community. In competitive pitches, competing agencies would always bring that up, and implicitly or explicitly ask the prospective client, "With McCann having Coke, how much attention do you think you're going to get from their best people on your (smaller, and less important) account?" We fought it, but it was hard to overcome. The truth was that a great deal of the creative work for Coke, including the famous "Mean Joe Green" spot, was done in New York. New York also bought Coke's national media for them, as well as taking care of other tasks. The U.S. account was truly split between the two offices, with high-level executives working in both cities, as well as in two hundred countries around the world. As someone described it, Coke was like "an octopus with a thousand arms; no one person could even see all of them, let alone coordinate or control all of them."

There were about one hundred people at McCann Atlanta, and we billed approximately fifty million dollars, depending on how one cost-accounted Coke's billings. Georgia-Pacific was moving into town as a significant account. We also had Continental Telephone Company, primarily a rural carrier; Lockheed, a huge military aircraft producer; Six Flags Over Georgia, the amusement park; and Chick-fil-A, the number three fast-food chicken chain in the country.

Started in Atlanta, Chick-fil-A was growing rapidly and was in thirty-five states by 1981. Their main product was, and remains, the Chick-fil-A sandwich, a chicken breast served on a hamburger bun, always with a slice of pickle. The chicken was covered with a special coating, then deep-fried in peanut oil that made it extremely tasty. Once they tried it, people raved about it, and always came back for more. The advertising was designed to get people to try it just once, then the sandwich would sell itself. The advertising theme was, "Taste it, you'll love it for good." We delivered a lot of coupons, and their operators—called franchisees in other food systems—were encouraged to pass out samples to passersby.

Chick-fil-A was growing at a rapid rate, but its growth was slowed by a few major factors. The founder and owner, Truett Cathy, was fiscally conservative. He wouldn't borrow money, so all growth was funded from internal cash flow. And the company stores were only located in shopping malls, with no free-standing units until later in the early '80s. But most importantly, Mr. Cathy was a very religious man and wouldn't allow his stores to open on Sundays, a big shopping day for malls. And to his credit, Mr. Cathy has kept all his stores closed on Sundays to this day, even though that policy initially kept Chick-fil-A from being admitted to some malls.

Georgia-Pacific was our second-largest account after Coke. The VP of Marketing at G-P was Steve Johnson, who had formerly been the manager of the McCann-Erickson office in Portland. He was a smart, talented client, who knew the agency business and helped the advertising process along with good direction. One of the first things G-P did when it decided to move back to Atlanta—it had originally been formed in Georgia, hence the name—was to sponsor the PGA tournament that was held in Atlanta every year. The Georgia-Pacific Classic was played every June at the Atlanta Country Club. It enabled the company to get its name around town in a favorable light, as it raised money for Atlanta's leading children's hospital. G-P had also constructed a huge "signature" building in downtown Atlanta, as it made its presence known.

John Malley was the account supervisor on several of Georgia-Pacific's brands, as well as their corporate image campaign. When I arrived at McCann he was serving as part of the "rear guard" in Portland, waiting to move back to Atlanta, along with the last contingent of G-P's marketing department. For the first six months of working with him, I only knew John through a speakerphone. He was an excellent account man, constantly thinking up creative ways to promote his clients' products. Along with some other brands, John also directed G-P's corporate campaign. That one used the usual strategy for a "conglomerate" with a lot of natural resources. The commercials portrayed G-P as a large, multiproduct company that managed its vast natural resources—coal, oil, timber, etc.—very prudently.

Late in 1981 John and his wife moved back to Atlanta from Portland, as the final wave of G-P people arrived. We immediately hit it off. John had grown up in New York and had gone to college at Arizona. He fondly recalled being a classmate of Geraldo Rivera, whose name at the time was Gerry Rivers, he told us. We all worked especially hard on Georgia-Pacific's corporate campaign, as this was to be McCann Atlanta's first effort after G-P had moved to town. Much of the campaign had been created under the direction of Len Farber. Len was the Creative Director of McCann Atlanta, having moved into town with the rest of the contingent from Portland. Prior to his Portland assignment, Len had been with McCann offices all over the world, including Europe, South America, and the Caribbean. He was a talented creative type, but also a good businessman. We hadn't met while I was interviewing because Len had been away. But since then we had had several good conversations about how the creative and media departments were supposed to work together, but often didn't.

It was true. The creative guys always wanted to produce long, exotic TV commercials that would run on the top-rated primetime programs. Media people often made them face the fact that the available budget was better spent on shorter-length commercials that would run in less-expensive time periods, such as early morning and late night. Or the media department would, heaven forbid, recommend that radio or magazines be used instead of TV. And if magazines were to be employed, the creatives wanted to do full-page, four-color spreads, and the media planners wanted to use small-space black-and-white ads. It was the age-old battle of grandiose ads that provided impact versus more modest ads that were efficient. Len and I agreed that there could always be a happy medium between the two, and we put that thinking into practice. Len and I worked well together throughout my stay at McCann, and we remain good friends today. We had our battles, but it was always on a professional basis, not conducted to see who could control the biggest amount of territory or feed his ego the best.

The G-P corporate campaign was a case in point. We had enough money to buy TV and magazines, but we were very particular in our media selection. Since we were seeking to reach upscale business executives and people who owned stocks, we bought upscale news and sports programming on TV, and highly targeted magazines with smaller circulations—and lower page rates—than the mass-circulation publications.

As with most corporate campaigns, G-P's was heavily scrutinized by the company's top management, and was run by the CEO for final approval. The marketing department at G-P approved the campaign first, as they were involved in its development. To get final approval, it had to go up the ladder through several layers of top management. This included operations and financial executives, who typically don't have much experience in advertising.

Corporate image campaigns always made for an interesting process, as the storyboards and media summaries made their way up the corporate hierarchy. They had to pass through executives who hadn't been involved in the development of the campaign, and who usually had no background knowledge of how the strategies, then the specific ads had evolved. The agency had to go through a lot of layers, where many could say "no," but couldn't give final approval by saying "yes." Most CEO's served as the final judge on corporate image campaigns for many reasons, including the fact that that's what their friends at the country club would be commenting to them about. And it was, if successfully placed, one of the most visible parts of their company, both to the public and their friends.

So working a corporate image campaign through the executive ranks outside the marketing department is always an adventure, often conducted in uncharted waters. The agency has to get approval for the campaign from important people who often know little about advertising, and who normally don't know the agency very well. It requires a great deal of diplomacy and salesmanship.

For one meeting Chuck and John went over to show the campaign to the top operations executive at G-P. The man had a reputation as a tough, bottom-line oriented member of G-P's management team. He knew how to run mills and turn out product efficiently, but very little about advertising. They anticipated trouble, and got it. I happened to be in Elliot's office when they returned at six o'clock, two hours later than expected. Chuck stopped to drop off his briefcase in his office next door, and John walked in with a weary look on his face. "How'd it go?" asked Elliot. John, in less than his usual cheery manner, answered, "Well, I got blood on my briefcase, but he approved it." After that meeting, the campaign continued up the ladder to the top, was ultimately approved, and ran for several years with "fresh" commercials every now and then.

Chuck, always good with words, picked up on John's description of the meeting, getting "blood on my briefcase." He spread it around the agency, and it became a codeword for how meetings with clients had gone. After a meeting, instead of asking, "How'd it go?" Chuck and everyone else would ask the participants, "Get any blood on your briefcase?" If the answer was "no," it was understood that the meeting had gone well, with the recommendation being approved. An answer of "yeah," was always followed by an explanation of what had gone wrong, usually ending with an expletive about the client's inability to recognize good advertising. While not as concise as Caesar's "veni, vidi, vici," the phrase served as shorthand to describe client meetings for months afterward.

When we left Haddonfield we had priced our house aggressively and listed it with the top real estate firm in the area. We thought it would sell easily, as it was in good condition and had a unique characteristic—it was built on the highest piece of ground in Haddonfield. But nothing was enough to overcome the highest mortgage rates in years. They shot up to 17-18 percent, and stayed there for months. Karen and I had found a beautiful house in Atlanta that we bought at a 17.5 percent interest rate. At the same time we got a swing loan at 12 percent from a bank in Haddonfield to use for the down payment. It was a stupid move, as it turned out, because our house didn't sell, even though we lowered the price.

After nine months we were tired of paying two mortgages and the swing loan, and every time the phone rang we ran to it, hoping it would be an offer. It never came, and we were scraping the bottom of our financial barrel to make our three monthly payments. Because I had come into the McCann system from the outside, I wasn't eligible for Interpublic's moving package, which included buying a transferees' house, thereby relieving him from the possibility of paying for two houses at the same time. I went to see Elliot and laid my cards on the table. I explained our situation and told him, half-jokingly, that McCann could either pay for our house in Haddonfield, or our psychiatric bills.

He understood our problem and said he'd go to bat for me with the right people in New York. The next day I got a copy of a memo Elliot had written to the head of Human Resources in New York, explaining my situation, and advocating that I become eligible for the transfer package. His rationale was that I had now been at McCann for nine months, was working out well, and had been caught in an unusually harsh housing market, due to the prevailing mortgage rates. The powers in New York agreed, and we sold our house to McCann's real estate company for a reasonable price, avoiding the psychiatrist's couch. I have been grateful to Elliot ever since, knowing that he not only went to bat for me, but hit a home run.

CHAPTER THIRTEEN

"Coke Is It" Meets "The Pepsi Challenge"

Coca-Cola dominated Atlanta in many ways in 1981, and still does today. Their sphere of influence includes Emory University, which has billions of dollars in Coke stock in its endowment fund. It also covers SunTrust Bank, which holds several billions in stock, as well as Coke's secret formula in its vault. It holds the attention of thousands of Atlanta residents whose major asset is Coke stock, as well as the thousands who work for Coke or its suppliers. Its employees live in all parts of the city, and Coke not only contributes to highbrow causes such as the symphony, but also buys scoreboards for high school and Little League fields all over town.

Coke's influence also pervades McCann-Erickson, not only the New York and Atlanta offices, but also its other offices around the world. When Coke began building plants and selling product in China, McCann followed it in, opening offices in Beijing and other cities as Coke expanded. McCann acquired the account in 1954, and right then entered the cola wars against Pepsi. McCann Atlanta does some work for Coke's national campaigns, but the main campaigns, such as "Have a Coke and a Smile," typically come from the New York office.

In Atlanta we worked on Coke's fountain business—fast food, theaters, and other outlets where Coke is poured for the customer— as well as sports and special event advertising. The McCann executives who worked on Coke internationally also officed in Atlanta, but they were abroad so much that we only saw them occasionally.

One of the senior international account directors was a tall friendly Australian named Paul Hammell. He and I hit it off well, as I knew a lot about Australia and had several friends there. And Paul was an outgoing and boisterous Aussie, similar to Texans in their hardworking, hard-playing demeanor. One day a group of us returned to the office after a long lunch, celebrating the approval of a big campaign. Paul had joined us, even though our victory didn't involve Coke. The lobby of the building was almost deserted, except for a few customers going in and out of the bank, which shared the building's lobby. While we were waiting for an elevator, Paul broke into song, bellowing out a raucous version of Australia's favorite ditty, "Waltzing Matilda." The policeman who guarded the lobby and the bank called across the lobby to Paul, and said, "Sir, you need to stop singing."

Paul stopped singing, looked over at the policeman, and asked mischievously, "Or what?"

"Or I'll arrest you," answered one of Atlanta's finest.

"Oh, come on, Mate, you wouldn't do that just for singing, would you?"

"Don't try me," said the cop, as he walked over to Paul.

Some of us quietly indicated to Paul that he should be careful, but he broke out with another verse. He didn't finish it, as the policeman slammed him against the wall and had him cuffed before Paul knew what hit him. The cop called on his shoulder radio for a car to come take Paul downtown. This sobered the rest of us very quickly, and despite our pleas, Paul went for a ride. We got him bailed out later that evening, but the fun lunch was over. I guess Paul learned his lesson, as I never heard of him getting in trouble with the law again, even though he kept up his Aussie spirit of fun.

Another character in the office was an account man on Continental Telephone named Jack Androsky. Jack had graduated from Harvard, and didn't let you forget it, always mentioning it within five minutes of meeting someone new. After hearing that, most people thought Jack would be intelligent, and perhaps he had academic smarts, but he hardly knew to come in out of the rain. He looked smart, but did dumb things. Secretaries hated him because he'd hand them sheets of legal paper with his handwritten scribbles, and told them to type it up. It looked like Chinese writing with arrows directing where paragraphs were to start and end. It took a cryptographer to decipher it, and slowed him down as secretaries misread his scratches and had to correct them, often several times. Jack didn't listen to anyone when we told him to just write a little better, or get a dictating machine. He felt it was their responsibility to decipher his gibberish, no matter how bad it was.

Looking back and playing amateur psychiatrist, maybe Jack just had a low regard for women, or maybe he just liked to humiliate them. This trait may have shown itself in his relationship with one woman. Eight blocks north of McCann's office was one of Atlanta's premier strip joints—or gentlemen's clubs, depending on your orientation—the Cheetah III. It was so close that one of McCann's junior copywriters danced there on a part-time basis. A group of us would go there every once in a while, either for lunch, or on Friday after work.

Jack was part of the group, and since he didn't have a wife or steady girlfriend, he was always more than willing to go. Later, he got a girlfriend, and was soon leading the charge to the Cheetah, as his girlfriend was one of the dancers. While most of us went there once every few weeks, Jack began going there almost every day for lunch or a drink after work. He soon had his own table, which he was proud to show off when he could convince a few colleagues to go with him. His girlfriend's name was Tammy, and Jack treated her like a princess, even while "sharing" her with all the other leering men in the place.

One day about four of us answered Jack's plea to join him at the Cheetah for lunch. It was hard to ignore, since every day at 11:30 he'd start calling for accomplices to go with him. Most of us would decline, but every once in a while some of us would join him. After all, it was only eight blocks away, there was no cover charge, and you had to eat lunch somewhere. We arrived, and Jack led us to his table. We all ordered a beer and a sandwich. Tammy came off the stage and pulled up a chair next to Jack. During a lull in the music, we heard him saying to her, "Yeah, I'll pick you up at seven and we'll go to Vinnie's." Just then, the stage announcer boomed over the microphone, "Come on boys, let's get these girls up on your tables. Special right now, table dances for five dollars." Jack immediately whipped out a five, gave it to Tammy, and said, "Come on, honey, give the fellas a table dance." Tammy took the bill, unsnapped her top, jumped on the table and ground out a dance to "Woolly Bully." We all enjoyed the dance, but began to wonder about Jack even more. The joke started that he'd marry Tammy, and then one night at a dinner party somewhere, perhaps with his boss present, Jack would have Tammy give the guests a table dance between courses. It was amusing to imagine, but Jack and Tammy eventually broke up.

At the other end of the morals spectrum was our client, Chick-fil-A, owned and staffed by very religious people, many of them born-again Christians. They didn't smoke, drink, or swear. As their agency, neither did we while in their presence. Sometimes we slipped, however, and let out a "damn" or "hell" in a meeting. They'd generally let it slide, but we always thought they were marking us down on a score sheet somewhere. Keeping it down the straight and narrow was fairly easy for a morning or afternoon meeting, and we could handle an occasional dinner without cocktails or wine.

But our limits were tested every year when Chick-fil-A would hold its annual operator meeting, which lasted five days. As their agency, we attended the entire meeting and presented the upcoming campaign to their management and several hundred operators. The good news was that these annual meetings were always held in very nice venues—a Caribbean island, for example. The bad news was that we were expected to be on our best behavior for the entire five days. There was no escaping into the night after dinner either, as there were religious speakers and prayer meetings right after each evening meal.

One year we all went to the Greenbrier, the resort of the

presidents, in West Virginia. The Greenbrier is a magnificent place, steeped in tradition and formality, where even today gentlemen are required to wear jackets and ties to meals, and ladies are "encouraged" to wear their nicest finery. Chick-fil-A's contingent, while large, didn't fill the place, but they requested that all the bars be closed down during their stay. As accommodating as the Greenbrier always tries to be, their answer was: we won't inconvenience our other guests by closing our bars; if you don't want to use them, simply don't go into one. It seemed like a reasonable response to most of us.

The McCann contingent was joined by Chick-fil-A's longtime public relations firm, Cohn & Wolfe, one of Atlanta's premier companies in that field. Their group was headed by Joe Osterhous, an experienced PR man, well respected by C&W's other clients, including Coca-Cola. Joe had a few of the other C&W staffers with him who worked on the Chick-fil-A account. There were about ten of us from McCann, including the two account executives who arrived a day after the meeting began, bringing the final completed creative materials with them.

We were scheduled to present the upcoming advertising and PR plans on the fourth day of the assembly. We'd meet in a bar after all the after-dinner sermons had been given to discuss our presentations. We always got a table out of view from passersby, as we didn't want to be seen by any of the Chick-fil-A people. It wasn't hard to get any table we wanted, since some several hundred of the Greenbrier's guests weren't utilizing the bars. When we broke up at the end of the evening, we all felt like high-school kids sneaking home and hoping our parents wouldn't catch us.

Another clash of cultures occurred the next night at dinner. Bill Cook, another senior executive at C&W, was right out of the Rodney Dangerfield mold, both physically and in his demeanor. He could be charming and abrasive, sometimes at the same time. Bill flew in especially for C&W's presentation, which was scheduled for the next day. Bill was a tough Brooklyn boy, who was almost totally insensitive of Chick-fil-A's morals and language preferences.

He also hovered on the fringes of the Greenbrier's dress code, showing up in a loud brown and orange leisure suit. He was seated at a table of ten, as we all were. The idea was for everyone to sit at different tables at each meal, so as to get to know as many people as possible. Each table had a "host," usually one of the Chick-fil-A executives from its Atlanta headquarters. The host of Bill's table that night was one of the founder's sons, Bobby. The host's main duty was to stimulate conversation at the table, to make sure that everyone met and got to know each other better. As the salad was being served, Bobby addressed the entire table. "Let's go around the table and all talk about the most fun thing we've ever done. Bill," he said, nodding at the man in the bright leisure suit, "what's the most fun you've ever had?" Without hesitation, Bill answered, "With one woman, or two?" The rest of the dinner went very well, with everyone acknowledging that they knew each other much better at the end of the evening.

The next day, both McCann and Cohn & Wolfe gave their presentations successfully. The new campaign was themed, "We Start Fresh Every Day." As with all our campaigns for Chick-fil-A, it was designed to generate trial of the product, then rely on its great taste to gain the repeat business. The prior tagline, "Taste It. You'll Love It for Good" wasn't totally abandoned, continuing to be used in direct mail ads and a few other places.

A few months after the Greenbrier meeting, Karen and I were blessed with the birth of our third child. We expected a third boy, but got a beautiful little girl, whom we named Sarah. She was born about two o'clock in the afternoon, thoughtfully allowing us to admire her appropriately, and then call "the list" during happy hour. Sarah was our third and last. All of them were "corporate" babies, having been paid for by Tracy-Locke, Campbell Soup, and McCann-Erickson. All three were born healthy and adapted well to the uncertainties of living in an agency family, which, as it's said, rarely wins the lawn-of-the-month award.

During this time Coke and McCann had been working on a new campaign. Pepsi had been attacking Coke with its "Pepsi

Challenge," in which people were blindfolded, given a taste of Coke and Pepsi, and asked which one they preferred. The "Pepsi Challenge" was meeting with success in some markets, taking share from Coke. Coke recognized the problem and knew that because of its sweeter taste, Pepsi was most often preferred in blind tests. But blind tests are unfair, in that when people normally drink (or eat) something, they know what it is. The expectation of what it's **going** to taste like influences how it actually tastes. Since Coke outsells Pepsi, the company knows that under normal circumstances, most people prefer it to Pepsi.

And speaking of normal circumstances, Coke's marketing executives and their agencies always remember that soft drinks, including Coke, are used by people for more than just quenching thirst. It's a "social lubricant" for many people, especially those too young to drink alcohol. The heaviest consumers of soft drinks on a per capita basis are people twelve to twenty-four years old. These people are the target audience for most Coke campaigns, and their habits, lifestyles, and feelings are studied by Coke in great detail.

From this knowledge, lots of strategic thinking and extensive consumer testing came the new slogan for Coke. After days of speculation and rumors that always precede a new Coke campaign, the new slogan was revealed. "Coke Is It" was the payoff line for a much deeper appeal to the target audience. Coke was portrayed as having a big, bold taste, so you knew you were really drinking something, and would be satisfied when you finished it. And what "it" was, was left to the consumer to decide, making the statement even more powerful.

The commercials cost millions to produce, and millions more would be spent to air them. While it might seem that money is no object when it comes to producing a campaign like this, there are people watching the costs. One that comes to mind is Coke's TV production director. Most big advertisers employ someone in that capacity, or hire them as needed. Their job is to review TV commercial storyboards before the spots go into production and look for ways to keep costs down. This might be as significant as questioning why the commercials have to be shot in London instead of Los Angeles, or as simple as asking if a kitchen set really needs a refrigerator.

Coke's TV production manager had been a TV producer and knew all the tricks of the trade. Besides finding specific ways to reduce the cost of a commercial, she was very forceful in her dealings with creative people and directors. This "intimidation factor" also held costs down, as those people knew she was watching, and they didn't go overboard in the way they planned their commercials. I always thought it was strange that someone would be worrying about savings of five thousand dollars here and there, while millions were being spent overall, but someone had to make sure that the creatives didn't have a blank check.

"Coke Is It" was first introduced at a convention of all the Coke bottlers that was taking place in Atlanta. They were wined and dined one evening, then shown the new commercials and given the plans for the new campaign. While they were all inside the Atlanta Civic Center, outside there was a big change going on. Coke had arranged for all the Coke billboards in Atlanta to be changed over to the "Coke Is It" copy during the dinner and presentation. In Atlanta, that's a lot of billboards, but they were ready when the bottlers emerged and walked or took cabs back to their hotels. "Coke Is It" served its purpose and remained the slogan for several years.

Sometime after this, Coke's Atlanta bottler—it was an independent bottler at the time, not owned by Coca-Cola—tried a new campaign. It was called "Coke in the Morning," and was just what it sounds like. The idea was to add a new time of day for drinking Coke, thereby increasing overall consumption. It didn't seem all that farfetched to me, as I remembered lots of people in Dallas drinking their Dr. Pepper as they drove to work. We bought morning drive time on almost every radio station in Atlanta. It did increase sales, and it was eventually expanded into some other markets, where it ran for a few years, then died out. The increased volume simply didn't justify the cost of generating that volume.

About this time we got the opportunity to pitch the AmSouth

Bank account. The bank was a major one, headquartered in Birmingham, and was firing its Atlanta agency. Elliot took charge of this effort, and put together a team consisting of Len Farber for creative, Jake Raucher for account service, some research people, and me. I brought along our head media buyer, who was great at showing how much broadcast we bought in the Southeastern markets. Clients loved to hear about "clout," that great myth that equated how much an agency spent in various markets with its competence level.

We drove to Birmingham in two cars, gave our credentials presentation, and presented some preliminary positioning and advertising ideas for AmSouth. Everything clicked, including the chemistry, and we were awarded the account a week later. Our primary client contact was Tim Mulcahy, director of advertising. Tim was a great client—very smart, marketing savvy, and agency-friendly. Every time he'd come to Atlanta for a meeting, a long happy hour took place, followed by a great dinner somewhere, and often some late-night carousing—after a full day of meetings, of course. We had a good, long relationship with AmSouth, and we spent a lot of time in Birmingham and other Alabama markets. I always enjoyed my time there, but I saw firsthand how Alabama became Georgia's whipping boy. A long-running riddle provides insight as to how Atlantans knock their Alabama neighbors:

Q: What's the best thing to come out of Alabama?
A: Interstate 20.

Another memorable event for everyone at McCann and in Atlanta came in the winter of 1981-82. A rare snowstorm was blowing in across Alabama. We had been talking to Tim and some other clients in Birmingham, who warned us that a storm had hit them around lunchtime, and that it was a big one. That meant more than two inches of snow, according to Atlanta standards. As the afternoon progressed, the skies became grayer, and flurries began. By four it was coming down hard, and Elliot closed the office.

What no one knew was that the "flurries" had turned into an ice storm.

A few people got out before the bad part of the storm hit. Most of us weren't too concerned and started drifting out. By 4:30 downtown Atlanta was an ice patch, with cars sliding and smashing into each other on every block. I tried to drive my Mustang, but couldn't even get out of the parking garage. I reparked and headed back up to the office. There were about fifty people still there, standing or sitting around in groups of five to ten. A group of us met in Elliot's office. Looking down onto North Avenue from his sixth-floor window, we saw a car skid into another one and catch fire. We decided we couldn't get home for a while and broke out a bottle of scotch.

By this time it was about six o'clock and the storm had stalled traffic all over the region. We got calls from our spouses saying they were trapped somewhere, or wondering when we'd be home. Elliot's wife didn't think things were serious and accused all of us of just wanting to stay downtown and have a party. Around this time we ran out of scotch and found a volunteer to go down the street to one of our watering holes and pick up a variety of bottles. It was becoming apparent that we might be spending the night in the office, as the radio was reporting that hundreds of cars were abandoned on I-285, Atlanta's beltway. What would come to be known as "Snowjam '82" was in full swing. In a show of budding capitalism, students from Georgia Tech's downtown campus went from car to car, offering stranded motorists a can of beer, a cup of hot chocolate, or a hot dog for five dollars. The last of us were able to leave the office around 2:00 a.m. Elliot made sure everyone had found a ride home or a nearby hotel room, then drove several other people home; he dropped me off at 4:00 a.m. Tardiness the next day was tolerated very leniently.

A few months after this we were asked to develop a corporate image campaign for the Continental Telephone Company. Through a series of acquisitions the company had grown dramatically and was changing its name to Contel. We all agreed that this sounded more "high-tech" than the old name.

Contel was indeed a high-tech company. One of the things it did was provide the telecommunications equipment that enabled a fledging newspaper to transmit copy and advertising by satellite. That newspaper, just starting up in 1981, was *USA Today*. Their reps were calling on us and pointed out that fact. I passed it on to the Creative Department and suggested that it might make a good ad for Contel, with the idea of running it in *USA Today*, as well as other appropriate publications. As the first truly national newspaper carrying general news, the Gannett Company was generating a lot of "buzz" that Contel could use to its advantage. As with most ideas sent from media departments to creative departments, it was brushed aside and never used. McCann's Creative Department moved ahead with a high-energy, high-tech campaign that resembled the graphics in the movie *Tron* that had recently come out.

The corporate communications job at Contel had been filled by a new person, Virginia Lee. She had been involved with the name changes for several companies, which isn't as simple as it sometimes seems. The new name has to be thought of, agreed to by top management, and often the board of directors. Legal searches have to be made to secure the name, a new logo has to be created, and company letterhead and signage changed, among other tasks.

At the same time an advertising campaign has to be developed that will favorably impact the company's customers, employees, shareholders, and investment community. It's a major undertaking, which is why companies generally appoint a very senior person to head up the process. Bringing in a brand-new executive is somewhat unusual, in that there are often sensitive issues that are best addressed by someone familiar with the "old way" of doing things as the "new way" is brought in. Bringing in Virginia Lee, with this as her first main assignment, made us even more wary than agencies usually are when a new marketing or communications executive comes on board.

Our fears were soon realized. Ms. Lee had apparently been told, or had decided on her own, to throw the account up for grabs, to be decided by an agency review. This wasn't too much of a surprise, as companies often use a name change to take a look at alternative agencies. What was surprising, demoralizing, and maddening was the fact that we learned of the review from the ad column in *The New York Times*. Even though we had had several meetings with her, and felt we were at least beginning to gain her confidence, she had chosen to blindside us with the review.

Of course, Elliot called Virginia immediately, and asked what was going on, and why we hadn't been warned. "I wanted to make it fair for everyone," was her answer. That was telling, meaning she had no allegiance to us, and we hadn't earned much, if any, of her confidence. We knew we were in for a fight to keep the business.

Eliot and Len Farber, our creative director, flew to New York to see Edward Williams, the dynamic chairman of Contel. Mr. Williams was the driving force behind Contel, having put together a combination of small, rural telephone companies into a large, high-tech communications giant. They tried to go over Virginia Lee and head off the review, but to no avail. He made it clear that she was operating with his blessing, and that he wouldn't step in, despite our association with Contel for several years. Despite our best efforts, including a terrific creative campaign, we lost the contest.

There was the usual griping, blaming, and second-guessing after an agency loses a battle to **keep** an account. It's always more intense than the self-flagellation that comes after not **winning** an account. We conducted a postmortem and concluded that Virginia Lee's agenda had been to get rid of us from the start, probably under the orders of the Edward Williams, as part of a clean sweep. We could never determine the real reason. And our new general manager, Cliff Howell, who replaced Elliot a short time later, missed a real opportunity to find out what had taken place. Virginia Lee was fired from Contel a few months after we were fired. We couldn't believe it, but she then had the audacity to call Cliff, looking for a job or some leads. Cliff, of course, told her he was much too busy to have lunch with her. In retrospect, most of us wish he would have taken her to lunch, and perhaps found out what her real orders and motivations had been.

It was around this time that I had an experience that's never been duplicated since. A few of us from McCann were having dinner with a couple of reps from *Forbes*. We were dining at Bone's, one of Atlanta's top restaurants, and a big advertising hangout. Bones is famous for its friendly atmosphere, as well as its great steaks. Someone once described it as "a club without dues." Most people who went there, regulars or first-timers, regard other patrons as fellow "members." When conducting business in Atlanta, Bones is one of the main stops on the good ol' boys network.

We were having a few drinks in the bar before dinner. As it started to get crowded, we offered a barstool to a large man who had been standing behind us. He was alone and appeared to be waiting for others. Tom, one of the regular bartenders who serves as "master of ceremonies" when he's on duty, introduced Bob to our group, mentioning that he was visiting from Chicago. Since I was closest to him, I welcomed him to Atlanta and Bones and asked if he'd been to either before. He said yes to both, and that he was in town for the Beef Producers convention. We continued to talk, and he told me he was the marketing director for the Independent Beef Processors Association, a trade group that promoted the consumption of beef. I was familiar with their campaign, "Beef. It's What's for Dinner," that was running on radio and TV. I told him who we were, and we had one of those friendly, but cautious barroom discussions, where you want to appear intelligent, but are careful not to give away any secrets to someone you just met.

During our talk, Bob mentioned that he had checked out an agency in Atlanta as a possible addition or replacement for one the IBPA was currently using. He had stopped in at the agency earlier that day, totally unannounced and unscheduled. He said that was the way he evaluated potential agencies that he had checked out "on paper" beforehand. He also stated that the agency he visited had not impressed him. Most agency evaluations involve formal presentations, and sometimes even speculative work, usually arranged weeks in advance. I asked Bob why he conducted his evaluations by simply "popping in" unannounced. His response was surprising to me at first, but made a lot of sense. "I see how the agency's receptionists react to the situation. The way they respond tells me how important the agency considers its 'public face' to be. Are the receptionists tied in with the rest of the agency, or are they just office 'guards'?"

"That doesn't seem too relevant to their other abilities," I responded.

Bob continued: "Yeah, but it's an early indication. When I tell them that I'm a prospective client, it's interesting to see who they call to come meet me. Sometimes it's the president, sometimes it's an administrator or a secretary. How the person who comes out to meet me reacts is also very telling."

"What if the president's out of the office," I asked.

"That's even more informative. I get to see how the agency runs when the big dog isn't around. When I tell them the size of our account I eventually get to the person in charge at the moment, and see how they react. Are they flustered, do they call in additional executives, do they drop everything, do they palm me off to the new business person?"

"You make some great points. I've never seen or heard of that method."

"If I like the way the agency reacts, I can always come back in a few weeks to see their canned presentation, and their well-rehearsed pitch. But before that, I've caught them in their everyday routine, and seen how they handle the unexpected."

I told him that I was with McCann-Erickson, and I invited him to drop by the next day and check us out. Bob said he was leaving the next day and couldn't come by. I got his card, and we shook hands, as his guests arrived. We followed up with him, but we couldn't get him to pay us a visit, scheduled or unscheduled. Even so, his method of meeting and evaluating agencies intrigued me, and I decided if I ever became a client again I'd try it someday.

Sometime after this the Atlanta Advertising Club had Charles Osgood as the monthly speaker. He was fantastic, in that he knew his audience, and gave a very meaningful talk. He spoke for forty-five minutes, and made several good points about the advertising industry in general, and media buying specifically. The most relevant point regarding media was one we'd heard many times before, but not from such a distinguished authority as Mr. Osgood. His point was that we made decisions about which media vehicles to use for our commercials based on numbers—how much the commercial costs, how many people it will reach, the cost-per-thousand viewers, etc. He said numbers are important, but they don't tell the real story about a medium and how its message is received by viewers or readers.

As an example of using numbers to substitute for what really happens, he cited a recent fire in Manhattan that his news colleagues at CBS had covered. "They reported that the fire went to **five alarms; eighteen trucks** responded, with over **one hundred firemen** involved. The fire burned out **six stories** of a **forty-seven-story** building, and caused damage in excess of **ten million dollars**." Mr. Osgood continued his talk by saying, "All these numbers were reported that night on the newscast, and the audience heard them as they watched the tape of the burning building. Then he drove his point home, saying, "But the real story was not in the numbers, not in how many alarms were sounded or how tall the building was. The real story is the trauma of the people who suffered from smoke inhalation, the tragedy of families being burned out of their homes, and the heroism of the firefighters who risked their lives to make sure everyone got out safely. Those are the things that really matter, and they don't show up in numbers." Mr. Osgood said it more eloquently than I'm able to reproduce it here, but it had a big impact on the audience, reminding us that we're in a business that depends on our ability to affect people's emotions. Though we often forget, in advertising the numbers are supposed to play second fiddle to our knowledge, judgment, and intuition about human behavior.

CHAPTER FOURTEEN

Wanda, the Wicked Media Queen

One of the best things about being in a media department is that you meet lots of different people in the form of media representatives. They come from all kinds of backgrounds and represent all kinds of media. They can be smooth and sophisticated, such as the typical network television salesman, or a little rough around the edges, such as a salesman for hunting magazines. In any case, media planners are charged with meeting media representatives, listening to their pitches, then deciding if their medium should be recommended to clients for use. Over the years some of the best people I've known, in or out of the business, have been media reps. Several of them have become lifelong friends, sometimes after hard-fought negotiations and other battles.

One of the best reps I've ever met is Mark Kiely, who now works for Time Inc. In the early 1980s Mark was with *Fortune* magazine, managing their Atlanta office. He had opened the office because of Atlanta's rising stature as a national headquarters city, not just a city for regional branches. *Business Week* and *Forbes* had had offices for years, with *Fortune* covering the city from Chicago. Mark quickly assimilated into the Atlanta advertising community via the usual means: making sales presentations to all the right people, holding lunches and after-work events for media planners, and socializing with leaders in the advertising community.

Mark was a good golfer, and enjoyed taking clients and agency people to play. One of our clients was Sam Dooner at MSA, who also loved to play. Mark had invited Sam to play a few times, usually going to dinner after the nineteenth hole. MSA, one of the leading software companies at the time, was using *Fortune* as part of its print campaign, so Mark felt pretty good about his relationship with Sam. He later told the story about just how good he felt about him. Mark's boss, Harry Jackson, was flying in from New York one afternoon, and wanted to meet Mike to discuss the possibility of even more business in a special Atlanta section in the magazine. This was a last-minute trip, so he called Mark from New York before he left, and asked him to get Sam for a meeting, drinks, and dinner that evening. "No problem," responded Mark, "I **own** him," using a dangerous term that is rarely true in advertising sales. Since his wife was out of town on an extended stay at a relative's house, Sam wouldn't need a "pass" to get out that night.

As Harry made his way down to Atlanta on the plane, Mark kept calling Sam's office to arrange a meeting that evening. Sam's secretary told him he was in a meeting, and Mark couldn't break through the protective shield. He was still trying as Harry arrived at his office at five o'clock, asking what the plans were for the evening. Mark explained his inability to reach Sam up to that point. "So much for owning him," responded Harry, who proceeded to needle Mark about it for the next few days. Even though it turned out that Sam really had been in an all-afternoon meeting, and had other plans for the evening, Mark learned his lesson and rarely claimed to "own" anyone after that. Luckily for him, he and Harry were good friends, and worked closely together at other Time Inc. magazines.

Mark told me another story that illustrates the degree to which some media planners think the media community owes them something. All of us in the business have accepted some kind of gratuity at one time or another, whether it be lunch at an expensive restaurant, theater tickets, or trips to faraway lands. Most of us recognize that these are "extras" that we're privileged to be given. But some media planners and buyers believe these perks are "owed" to them by the media because they spend a lot of money with them. These people are known by names such as "Media Queens,"

"Takers," or "America's Guests." The worst of them take everything they can get, go on every trip they can, then act like jerks.

I've seen many of these people in action myself. One client I know, Ron, ran a few pages in *Hunting* magazine, and as part of the deal was given a week at an exclusive hunting lodge in South Carolina. The idea was for him to invite a few of his best customers to enjoy a week of good hunting together. Instead, Ron took his family and a neighbor's family to the lodge. On top of that, they took side trips and ordered themselves extra equipment, charging over $2,500 to the *Hunting* magazine account. A month later, when the folks from *Hunting* got the bill and pieced together what had occurred, they had a choice to make: confront Ron and ask for repayment, jeopardizing future business from Ron; or let it go, and think twice about offering him anything in the future. They let it go, choosing not to confront him.

Mark's story is another example of a "taker" getting out of control. One year the PGA golf championship was held at Shinnecock Hills, about ninety miles outside of Manhattan on Long Island. *Fortune* had a hospitality tent at the tournament and had decided to entertain clients and agency people there, as golf and *Fortune* have similar demographics. Besides using limos to drive their guests out to Shinnecock, *Fortune* had contracted for two helicopters to move the most important people back and forth, avoiding the dreaded Long Island traffic. A notorious "media queen," an agency media director who didn't even play golf, was placed in the high priority group that would be choppered to and from the course.

During the day one of the helicopters developed mechanical trouble and had to be taken out of service. *Fortune* couldn't replace the chopper, but was quickly able to round up additional limos to take up the slack. Several of the top priority people who had flown out to Shinnecock were informed that they'd be driven back to the city via limo. There were a few that had drunk so much they didn't know the difference, but everyone accepted the change with no problem.

Everyone except Wanda, the wicked media queen. When Mark told her she would be riding rather than flying back, she protested immediately, using the logic that since she had flown out, she should fly back, never mind that one chopper had been disabled. Mark calmly explained the situation to her, but her protestations just grew louder and harsher, to the point where she threatened to never again place any of her clients' money in *Fortune*. When Mark heard that, he'd had enough, and simply said, "I'm sorry, do what you have to do." That was the smart thing to do, because if push came to shove, the *Fortune* sales staff could go to Wanda's clients and let them know why she was boycotting the magazine. Good clients are not interested in having their media dollars spent on personal vendettas. And many media directors forget that lots of media representatives, especially magazine reps, have close personal and professional relationships with clients.

Wanda was wise enough not to try to carry out her threat. But her behavior, unfortunately, is not all that uncommon among media executives, both on the client and agency side of the business. Agency media directors seem particularly vulnerable to becoming takers, and believing their own press about how important they are. As senior executives, they've had years of media representatives telling them how smart they are, as part of the selling process. Even when they don't make a schedule, most media reps treat agency media people with kid gloves, not wanting to jeopardize future possibilities. By the time they become media directors, many expect media reps to come in and kiss their rings, among other things. I've often thought that we should take a page from the Roman Empire in their glory days. When a successful Roman general rode in triumph through the streets of Rome to the cheers of the adoring crowds, a slave would stand beside him in his chariot. The slave would whisper constantly into the general's ear, "You are not a god, you are mortal." To a lot of media directors, including Wanda, such treatment would be totally appropriate.

Unfortunately, all magazine representatives aren't as good as Mark. One who comes to mind is Kevin Ketchum, who was based in Atlanta and represented a golf magazine for a few years. Kevin was a veteran of the business, but had bounced around even more than most magazine reps, probably due to his lack of judgment and "rough" exterior. One memorable story about him illustrates both those shortcomings. Our client, Georgia-Pacific, had become the title sponsor to Atlanta's premier PGA tournament, the Georgia-Pacific Classic. Naturally, they ran ads in golf publications.

Right after G-P moved to Atlanta, Kevin made a sales presentation to several members of their marketing department. He hadn't met anyone in the department before, but had set up the meeting on the strength of his golf publication, one of the industry leaders. The G-P conference room was filled with several male and female brand managers and support staff. Many of them had moved from the Portland area, and many were Canadians. Kevin knew this and began his presentation by asking a question: "Why do Canadians always do it doggie-style?" There was total silence as part of his audience squirmed slightly in their chairs. Kevin quickly answered his own question: "So they can both watch hockey at the same time." There was a little nervous laughter, but not much. He finished his presentation, oblivious to the cool response to his opening line.

As soon as he left, some of the women in the audience complained to the VP of Marketing, who hadn't attended the presentation. On hearing about, then confirming Kevin's little joke, he called Kevin's boss in New York and told him never to send him into G-P again. Until he ultimately left Atlanta for a job at another magazine, Kevin was *persona non grata* at G-P and a few other places in town.

In late 1982 I got a plum assignment for a week. McCann's Kingston, Jamaica, office was pitching the Jamaican Tourism account and needed a media plan for the United States. They had no real expertise in American media, so the McCann system called for another office to lend them that expertise, namely me. My assignment was to fly to Kingston, spend a week there writing a media plan, then present it to the Tourism Board's marketing committee. I thought about bringing along my wife, Karen, but she'd just had our beautiful little girl Sarah, so I went alone.

Delta took me from Atlanta to Miami, then on to Kingston. Jamaica was emerging from the control of a leftist government that had resulted in shortages of food and most other consumer products. Cars were abandoned on the streets where they had broken down, with no parts to repair them. The country was in shambles, but the Blue Mountains above Kingston were as picturesque as Ian Fleming had described them. The account person who picked me up at the airport reminded me that Fleming wrote many of his James Bond stories from his home in those hills.

We drove to the McCann office, which was in a building that reminded me of a garden apartment, with three stories, open balconies on each floor, no elevators, just stairs. I quickly found out there was also a water shortage in Jamaica. The toilets in McCann's office were unusable, due to lack of water, so everyone had to go home to answer nature's calls. And the electricity on the island went off every so often, usually at night. As one of the creatives told me, the government did it on purpose, just to show the population who was in control of things. It would usually go out for a while during important times, such as when the Super Bowl was on, so the maximum number of people would be affected.

The people in the office were a mixture of locals and expats, including British, Chinese, Panamanians, and a few Americans. The head of the office was an Englishman named Brian Hughes, an accomplished ad man who liked living in Jamaica. He had bought a huge house in the Blue Mountains, with a great view of Kingston, at an incredibly low price, due to many well-to-do people leaving the island while the socialists ruled. Brian also had three large attack dogs who roamed his property twenty-four hours a day, making sure the crime levels in Kingston didn't reach his place.

I arrived at the McCann office early the first day, and was briefed on the proposed campaign for the Tourism Board. It was judged that there wasn't enough money to produce and run television commercials, so magazines became the selected medium. Using print, we could target people likely to travel and take vacations outside of the United States Magazines provided the opportunity to portray the beauty of Jamaica's beaches and other attractions, while at the same time delivering the upscale, adventurous audience that traveled outside the country. And with titles such as *Travel & Leisure, National Geographic, Diversion,* and other similar magazines, it was possible to place the advertising in an editorial environment that included exotic places, travel tips, and beautiful pictures of foreign lands.

McCann's creative team, headed by a young Panamanian, had produced some terrific ads, showing the picturesque beaches and the quaint sections of Kingston. And, of course, there were several ads featuring Montego Bay. Each one included the usual couple, young, handsome/pretty, and in love, enjoying the surroundings. After we discussed how and where the media plan would utilize these ads, it was time for lunch. Brian took several of us to lunch at the club where he belonged, which featured a huge verandah with overhead fans. As we sat under the slow-moving fans, drinking our Bloody Marys and Gin and Tonics, it seemed as if we could have been back in the days when Jamaica was a British colony.

After that first day I got down to business and spent the next few days developing a Year 1 media plan for Jamaican Tourism. Besides the beautiful ads in the glossy magazines I was reminded we also needed to plan for the black-and-white ads with the prices in them that ran in the travel sections of newspapers. As with a lot of "retail" ads, they weren't always pretty, but they sold a lot of trips.

The media plan was finished in a few days, so we started rehearsing for the final presentation to the Tourism Board. The agenda was to present an overview of the U.S. travel market, to show we knew all about it. Then the creative campaign, followed by the media plan, with time allotted for questions and answers. We rehearsed after business hours, then went out for drinks and a late dinner. On the morning of our presentation we all drove to a government building in downtown Kingston. I was amazed that there were small groups of goats running through the streets of the city. We unloaded our presentation materials—no electronic equipment, all easels and flip charts, in case we lost electricity.

We walked into an open courtyard, where twelve to fifteen men sat on bleachers, all dressed in dark pants and white shirts—the Tourism Board. After a few formalities and cursory introductions, we were "on." We gave our presentation smartly, with no questions asked by our audience. Either there was no time for questions and answers, or they didn't have any, as we were "dismissed" right after we finished. It was the most "sterile" audience reaction I've ever seen to an advertising pitch, which are often conducive to raucous reactions, emotional arguments, and confrontations—or they can be "lovefests," in which both parties practically cuddle with each other. This was the only one I've ever seen that might have been a trial, with no audience reaction allowed.

We celebrated that night anyway, and I flew back to Atlanta the next day. A few days later I got a nice note from Brian, thanking me for a good job, but informing me that McCann didn't get the business. It stayed with a local agency, and my cynical mind started to think that the whole contest had been a sham, probably required by the government, but with the outcome predetermined. I'd never find out, as there was plenty to worry about in the Atlanta office.

CHAPTER FIFTEEN

Who Says There's No Crying in Advertising?

It was 1985, and I'd been working for other people for fifteen years. I knew a lot about media, and I knew a lot of people. I had been thinking of starting a media planning and buying company for a year or two, and was mentally ready. I wanted a partner, and I knew who it was: Kim Kohler. We had worked together well for four years in Dallas, and had stayed in touch ever since. Kim had moved out to the Tracy-Locke office in San Francisco, then to Ogilvy & Mather in L.A. A few years later he moved back to Dallas and went to work for Frito-Lay as one of their top media people. As an illustration of just how small the advertising world really is, Kim's boss at F-L was Pam Kroll, whom I had worked for many years ago at Y&R New York. When Kim and I announced the creation of Kohler & Miller, Pam was most supportive.

We agreed to form the company during the spring of 1985, met in Atlanta to incorporate the business, and opened officially on July 1. Kohler & Miller seemed to roll off the tongue more easily than the other way around, so we agreed that "Kohler" would come first. In return, I got to be president, with Kim as executive vice president.

Were we scared? Yes. I had a wife, three kids, and a good-sized mortgage. Kim and his wife Liz had a baby on the way, and were moving to a strange town, outside of their beloved Texas. But we kept telling ourselves that we knew what we were doing, and were good enough to succeed. And we also kept saying that if we did fail, we were only in our midthirties, so we could get back to bigger companies, and resume our careers. About then we first heard the saying, "When you have your own business, you sleep like a baby—you wake up crying every few hours." Actually, once we made the decision to go ahead, the doubts and apprehension lessened, partially because of our self-satisfaction, and partially because we were so busy.

While we opened up without any clients, we soon had two—our former employers. Both hired us to work with them for two or three days a week, with Kim flying back and forth to Dallas. As time went on, we got more clients, but having work to do from day one was a big boost, even if it wasn't big bucks.

In order to save money we leased a three-office suite in Roswell, a growing suburb north of Atlanta, with much-lower rents than downtown. We committed only for a year, and bought some decent second-hand furniture. We hired a friend-of-a-friend to come in three days a week as our secretary. We did our own cleaning and took out our own trash. After paying ten cents a copy for a while we sprang for a copier. Fax machines weren't widespread, and computers were tremendously expensive, so we went without those, using an IBM Selectric for our typing needs. We didn't take salaries for four months, and then at a low level, but we were underway.

Our first client outside of our former employers was a hot young Atlanta agency, HilliardSmythe. We were hired to be their planning department, working in conjunction with their media buying group. As H-S grew, it needed more strategic media planning, and that's what we were hired to provide. We worked happily with H-S for a few years. Then they got their big chance. Southeast Bank in Miami, a big regional institution, was looking for a new agency, and H-S was in the hunt. Dan Hilliard recognized our contributions to their success, and we were glad to see them grow. They grew okay, and to Dan's credit he came to Kim and me prior to the Southeast pitch. He said that if they got Southeast the agency would be big enough to have its own media planning department, and that K&M would no longer be needed. Despite Dan's warning, we worked hard on the pitch, H-S won the business, and we were out the door. That was okay though, as Dan remained a good friend and supporter of ours, and sent us business as the situation warranted.

Later on we worked for Jiffy-Tune, owned by a self-made man who was as inflexible as a steel girder. We bought a lot of radio for Bob, designed to reach people in their cars so they could hear the spots, then turn immediately into a Jiffy-Tune for an oil change. Of course, people don't just decide to forget about where they're going and pull in for service, but Bob believed they did. So we bought very specific times on specific stations during morning and afternoon drive time. Because these were "fixed" in specific half-hours (compared to say, 3:00-7:00 p.m. in afternoon drive time) we ended up paying a premium for these positions. And since Bob was very religious, we bought spots only on noncontroversial stations—no Imus, no Howard Stern or other "shock jocks." That was okay, as clients are allowed to dictate their wishes once you've explained the implications of those dictates.

We always bought a high-rated country station in Atlanta, WKHX, known as "KICKS", with a popular morning host named Whale. Our spots were scheduled to run on Whale's show between 7:00 and 7:30 a.m., for which we paid a 30 percent premium over the regular 6:00-10:00 a.m. rate. One morning Travis Tritt, a hero in Atlanta, visited the Whale's studio for a short meeting that went long. Travis stayed around from 7:10 until 7:40, when he left. No way was the Whale going to interrupt an appearance by Travis Tritt, so the Jiffy-Tune commercial ran at 7:40, right after the interview. Bob refused to pay for the spot because it ran outside the established time period—even though being next to a Travis Tritt interview meant the audience was larger than expected. We negotiated a makegood and went on from there. Bob eventually ended up selling his chain of Jiffy-Tunes to Texaco, and I was glad I wasn't the negotiator for Texaco in that deal.

Another client we worked for was Chattem Consumer Products in Chattanooga. Chattem made Pamprin, Premisin, Mudd Mask, and several other high-profit products. One of those was BullFrog Sunblock, a new product they had purchased from a chemist in

California. The chemist had been worried about his son, a surfer, getting skin cancer. So he developed a formula that would provide a high SPF, and would not wash off in water, or "sweat off" during exertion on land. The chemist had started producing it in his garage, and like Panama Jack in Florida, BullFrog had taken off with the surfing crowd. From there it had spread to the surrounding sunny beaches and gained distribution in some chain stores. Always on the lookout for up-and-coming personal products, Chattem had purchased BullFrog and was in the process of taking it into national distribution.

One of the driving forces behind BullFrog was Frank Lane, head of a marketing consultancy in Atlanta. Frank was a former president of Neutrogena, and had also worked at P&G and S.C. Johnson. He had recognized BullFrog's potential and helped promote it via free samples in tiny packs called "Tadpoles." Frank was to serve as the brand manager for BullFrog as it was integrated into Chattem's marketing system. His challenge was to make sure it got special attention rather than being shuffled off to a junior brand manager, where it might die a slow death of neglect. Frank's presence was part of the sales deal for BullFrog, which stipulated that the sellers would get additional money if it met certain sales goals within Chattem's system.

As BullFrog was being integrated into the company, K&M was hired to take over the media planning and buying for all Chattem's consumer brands. We had the inside track with the new VP of marketing, an ex-Frito-Lay group brand manager. He had brought us in to plan and buy strategically, as opposed to the lowest cost-per-thousand method they'd been using for the last few years. They also wanted us to write a manual for their media policies and procedures, which they were revamping to more closely interact with their marketing plans. Chattem was a big piece of business for us, and both Kim and I worked on it.

Our philosophy regarding the role of media in the marketing mix was in tune with Frank's, and we hit it off right away. Together we formulated an advertising strategy for BullFrog that would enable it to break away from the established brands, as well as help in

Chattem's efforts to gain distribution in the major food and drug chains. We'd take the brand's tagline, "Won't Wet Off. Won't Sweat Off," and adapt it to various sports and other outdoor activities. Then we'd marry that with highly selective magazines that reached active people. BullFrog's message would be specifically directed toward runners, hikers, swimmers, volleyball players, campers, etc. The ads would then be placed in specific magazines to reach the group being addressed, such as *Runner's World, Backpacking,* and *Camping Journal.* The headlines would mention the activity for which the magazine was known, such as:

"Backpacking Without Burning"
"Camping Without Burning"
"Surfing Without Burning"

And so on. The copy talked about BullFrog's high SPF, and how it was perfect for the specific activity being discussed. For swimmers, it was strong enough not to wash (wet) off in the water. Then the ad would end with the tagline, "Won't Wet Off. Won't Sweat Off." To all of us it was a perfect marriage between the copy and the medium. Sales took off, and BullFrog continues to do well today.

Our relationship with Frank continued with other clients. A few years after we worked together with Chattem, Frank and a few partners, including a major food company, started a Chinese food delivery chain. It was called Mr. Ching, and was test-marketed in Atlanta. Mr. Ching's food was upscale Chinese-American, similar to the quality you'd find in the best Chinese restaurants.

The advertising for Mr. Ching was produced by one of Frank's colleagues on the West Coast. Virtually all the money was spent on radio, placed by K&M on stations in Atlanta with young, affluent listeners. The commercials featured a professor with a British accent, teaching his class to conjugate "Mr. Ching" as if it were a verb. "I Mr. Ching, You Mr. Ching, He Mr. Ching" was repeated over and over in the spot. The payoff line was, "For great Chinese food, ring Mr. Ching," followed by the telephone number. It was a hard-hitting, name-awareness ad. After hearing it a few times there was no forgetting "Mr. Ching."

We ran heavy levels of radio advertising on several major Atlanta stations, close to the levels of McDonald's. After about a week we got a call from the sales manager at one of the stations. They had received a few calls from some listeners, complaining about the tone and frequency of the Mr. Ching commercials. The sales manager wanted to know if we'd mind **reducing** the number of weekly ads on his station. This was the first and only time in my career that a media representative requested that we cut back the amount of spending with them. That's when we knew the commercials were working. But there were other problems to overcome.

Mr. Ching's food came in reusable bowls and was beautifully packaged with a Chinese emperor's seal around it. It was priced accordingly—expensive—and that contributed to its problems. A survey showed that Mr. Ching customers thought that the food was a little better than average Chinese takeout or delivered food, but they considered it too expensive. Further probing revealed that they really noticed the fancy dishes and packaging, and felt they were responsible for the "high" price. They resented paying "extra" for the dishes, when the traditional, "cheaper" cartons with handles were entirely acceptable.

The packaging was toned down and the Mr. Ching commercials continued running on the radio. But it was too late. Sales continued to miss the levels needed for profitability, as former customers would not retry the "new and improved" product. All of us advocated moving the test to another market, one that hadn't been "poisoned" by the old packaging, but the investors weren't willing to cough up more money. So Mr. Ching followed the Ming dynasty into history. But there are people in Atlanta that can still recall the "Ring Mr. Ching" commercials, proving once again that good advertising can't overcome a flaw in the product, or even a flaw in its packaging.

There were also opportunities to work with big agencies. In early 1987 we got a call from Valentine-Radford, a large, successful agricultural-oriented agency in Kansas City. One of the top executives there was an ex-Tracy-Locke account man, Charlie Ross, whom we'd kept in touch with since we parted ways. Through Charlie's consumer expertise, V-R had been awarded a small test campaign for Kansas City's biggest advertiser, Hallmark. V-R's media director had recently left, and while attempting to replace him, they needed media expertise for the test, which they expected to last four to six weeks. Since Kim had commuted earlier to Dallas and now had a young daughter, it was my turn to go on the road to Kansas City. I recalled my earlier visit there while at Y&R, and looked forward to returning.

Hallmark's test was for a new program they had developed, called the REACH program. While initially small, it was designed to ultimately stop an alarming trend with their business—their market share was declining, due to stronger traditional competitors, such as American Greetings and Gibson. Hallmark was also being hurt by the rise of smaller, "hipper" card makers, putting out funny, irreverent cards. Their situation was similar to Campbell Soup's, in that both had enjoyed a 75 percent plus share of market for ages, and was now being threatened by increased marketing muscle on the part of their traditional, smaller competitors, and growing "guerrilla" companies.

But Hallmark's distribution system differed from Campbell's because Hallmark had thousands of stores around the country, called Crown stores. They were owned and operated primarily by independent businesswomen and carried Hallmark cards exclusively. Hallmark was, in fact, responding to the cries of the Crown store owners to help fight the growing competition, which was hurting sales. From that situation the REACH program was developed.

Over the years Hallmark has become famous for its emotional, tear-jerking commercials that put a lump in your throat. They often appear in the long-running "Hallmark Hall of Fame" specials that air during the holidays. Most advertising critics believe those commercials to be among the best ever at invoking emotions from viewers, showing how card giving is more than just a ritual, and can be a real bonding experience between relatives and friends.

The REACH program, on the other hand, was to be a retail-oriented, make-the-cash-register-ring campaign. We planned radio and newspaper advertising to promote a free gift with the purchase of ten dollars or more in Hallmark's Crown stores. The promotions were planned around card-giving occasions, headed by Christmas, followed by Valentine's Day, Mother's Day, Easter, and graduations. Valentine's Day was to serve as our test period, and we ran the advertising in five test markets.

The response was overwhelmingly successful, above both goal and expectation. We knew we were on to something and expanded the market list to encompass an additional ten markets for the next phase, Easter. The free gifts were cuddly cotton bunnies that we thought women, the primary buyers of greeting cards, would find irresistible. And they did. Again, the test exceeded expectations, and we began planning to roll the REACH campaign into all of Hallmark's markets.

This resulted in me staying in Kansas City for four months instead of the original four weeks. Though I missed my family, it was good duty. I'd fly home to Atlanta every Friday afternoon, then go back to KC on Sunday night. I stayed in the Omni International Hotel, a modern inn with a pool on the top floor and two good restaurants. All my expenses were paid for, plus I was on a twenty-five-dollar food per diem, which enabled me to eat very well. Most nights I'd walk the eight blocks to the hotel from V-R's offices, go swimming, eat dinner in the hotel, and watch TV. Eventually, I got to know several people from V-R, and we'd occasionally hit bars and restaurants together. They were good people who worked hard and loved to root for the University of Kansas Jayhawks.

Working with the account team at V-R and the marketing people from Hallmark, we produced a presentation to give to all the Hallmark Crown store owners across the country. It explained the REACH program and solicited their participation in it. Three teams were set up to cover Hallmark's West Coast, Central, and Eastern regions. I served on the Eastern team, and we started our series of presentations, working our way to New York from Ohio.

We'd present to a few hundred Crown store owners in one city, then another a few days later.

Hallmark had a vested interest in making an effective presentation because they were asking each store owner to kick in for half the media cost of running the campaign, as well as paying for the gifts. Because the REACH campaign was expanded to the entire country, Hallmark didn't feel it could afford to foot the entire bill. So we were doing a selling job to the store owners to participate. Some were quite willing to kick in, while others were skeptical. This made for some raucous meetings, in which Hallmark's marketing department and the agency were harshly criticized. Part of the grousing didn't have anything to do with the REACH program, but the meetings served as opportunities for some owners to bash the company for other reasons. Some of it stemmed from frustration that Hallmark's share of the greeting card market was declining, and that was hurting their sales and profits. Even though the REACH program was designed to help reverse that decline, it was an opportune time to express displeasure with the "parent" company, and many did. We often found ourselves trying to defend more than just the upcoming advertising.

This phenomenon is common in franchise-type operations in many industries. It often results in the company firing the agency, in an effort to mollify the franchisees. It will usually hold them off for a while, but unless the real problem is fixed, the wolves will howl again. To Hallmark's great credit, its marketing and sales people faced the questions head on, and didn't try to shift the blame to V-R. The REACH program was implemented in all Hallmark markets with great success.

By the time the program had been rolled out to the Hallmark markets I had been at V-R for four months. I was flattered that they had asked me if I would be their media director, but I had respectfully declined. It was a great agency, with terrific people, but I didn't want to leave Atlanta or Kohler & Miller. Working with a headhunter in Chicago, I was able to help them find a qualified media director, from an Atlanta agency of all places.

On one of my last days in KC, Charlie Ross and I had a long

dinner together, and he told me a half-funny/half-sad story about their prior media director. Lonny Young had come in from the outside and taken over the department. He was a solid media tactician, but lacked good people skills. Instead of building a team, he seemed to scoff at the expertise of several members of the department, some of whom had been there for over twenty years.

They took it for about a year, then someone struck back. Lonny worked late one night, reorganizing the department on paper. He blocked out a new organization chart, shaking things up, including some surprise promotions and demotions. He also composed a chart that listed every member of the department, along with their current salaries and his proposed salary adjustments. Nothing too unusual, except that he left the organizational and salary charts out on his desk when he left. Nobody knew if he just forgot them, or figured he'd be in earlier than anyone else the next morning. In either case, someone, presumably a member of the department, found the paperwork. Whoever it was made copies of the salary chart, and placed one on the desk of every member of the department, as well as pinning it to the lobby bulletin board. That was the kiss of death, as salaries in agencies are widely divergent, and very confidential, for obvious reasons. Lonny left the agency shortly after that incident. That opened the door for me to come in and have a very enjoyable four months.

But not all such temporary duty in agencies is as pleasant as my experience with Valentine-Radford and Kansas City. A few years later I got a call from an agency in Atlanta, Ferra/Blue, who needed a media director to help on a big client they'd just landed. Ferra/Blue was owned by a woman whom I had worked with at McCann-Erickson, Jennifer Blue. She and her partner had left McCann and formed their own agency, specializing in fashion, cosmetics, and health and beauty aids. They were both extremely aggressive, attractive, and talented, so their business took off almost immediately.

They won several big pieces of business, and quickly added to their staff. At one point several years earlier they had hired us to help make a new business pitch to a division of Revlon in New

York, and we prepared for it over several weeks. We flew to New York, made a great presentation, but lost out to one of the big New York agencies. We were told later that the work done by Ferra/Blue was superior to anyone else's, but because the agency was so small, the marketing people were afraid to recommend it to upper management. But now Ferra/Blue had grown to over one hundred people and had earned a reputation as a leading health and beauty agency in the Southeast.

They had been awarded a forty-million-dollar hair care account, a division of an international conglomerate. Their product, called Golden Vision, competed with Clairol and L'Oreal, two well-established giants in the business. The agency was charged with developing a campaign that would get the Golden Vision message out, and invite women to call in or write in for a sample. The campaign had been tested in a few local markets, and was scheduled to roll nationally. But there was a problem to be addressed, in addition to how Clairol and L'Oreal would counter the introduction. The basic decision had not been made as to whether the Golden Vision campaign's primary objective was to generate a certain number of responses—via phone or mail—or to create awareness and trial of the product at the retail level.

It's generally not possible to successfully execute a "direct response" campaign and an "image" campaign with the same set of commercials. Sure, you can get a few people to call or write for the product with an image commercial, but rare is the direct response TV commercial that can enhance a product's image with consumers. In print, it's comparable to a small-space black-and-white newspaper classified ad compared to a beautiful, full-page four-color ad in a glossy magazine—they're both designed to elicit two different types of responses. The agency and client hadn't agreed on which response they wanted, partially because the Belgian parent company had insisted on "proof" that this huge forty-million-dollar expenditure was getting favorable consumer reaction. Sales and share-of-market were to take second place in importance to the cost-per-response of the TV and print campaign. The network TV, about thirty million dollars, had been committed on a wide variety of both broadcast and cable networks. Print ads totaling about ten million dollars, had been committed in women's fashion magazines and those serving teenage girls.

As the national campaign was about to start, Ferra/Blue's media director abruptly quit. I later found out that she had been driven out by the insensitive behavior of the two top Ferra/Blue account executives on the Golden Vision business. After months of nagging, hassling, and intimidating demands on poor Susan, they refused to let her take a long-planned vacation, so she quit. I didn't know this when Jennifer Blue called to see if I was available to be their acting media director for a few months while Golden Vision was launched nationally. At the same time she wanted me to help build a full-scale media department. Not knowing what I was getting into, I readily accepted the offer, and even gave them K&M's brother-in-law hourly rate.

I was to work at Ferra/Blue's offices fifteen to twenty hours a week, overseeing the media execution of the Golden Vision campaign, while recruiting, evaluating, and hiring additional media planners and buyers. At the same time, I'd make sure that K&M's clients were taken care of by my coworkers there, who needed little supervision. It looked like a great opportunity until I started to become familiar with the operating style of Sharon and Gail, the two account executives who had forced the prior media director to resign. My first indication of their M.O. came one evening as I was going over some media work with one of their subordinates. As we were discussing some solutions to a client request, the young lady's voice cracked all of a sudden, and she started crying, saying, "I can't do this anymore." At first I thought she was being funny, pretending that she was all stressed out. I almost started to join in, but before I did, I saw that she really **was** crying. "Deena," I said, "take it easy, it'll work out okay." In these days of sexual harassment charges, I declined to place her head on my shoulder, but I took one of her hands in both of mine and tried to comfort her. I suggested she go home and have a glass of wine, call her fiancé, and get a good night's sleep. She did, and thanked me the next day.

I thought her stress was just from working too hard, and worrying about her upcoming wedding. I soon learned that she, and the other members of the Golden Vision account service team, were being "managed" in the same way Susan, the media director had been—management by intimidation. They soon began treating my media people and members of the creative department the same way. They harassed competent, hardworking people that I had hired, and verbally abused them. They would agree to a deadline for a project to be completed, then arbitrarily move it up, as they piled on more assignments. Their main problem, besides not knowing how to motivate people, was that they were too insecure to say "no" to a client when the situation called for it. They'd nitpick every memo and report we prepared, causing everyone to resent them. One time they insisted we bring in an additional typist to retype forty pages of research that the agency had purchased. We could have simply summarized the research on three or four pages, but they believed in work "by the pound," and wanted to try to fool the client into thinking the research was original, rather than purchased from another firm.

Initially, we tried to roll with the punches, but the unreasonable demands and harassment never stopped, and there was never a compliment handed out. Even the people who worked for Sharon and Gail would try to temper their demands, but then they'd come down hard on their own subordinates. I saw another one of them sobbing uncontrollably in her office after they worked her over and denied her a vacation. At one point I told them we should alert Golden Vision to the spring upfront network TV buying process, which was approaching. They'd never heard of the "upfront marketplace," but tried to rewrite my presentation before we presented it to the client.

In twenty-five years of seeing and working for some pretty unreasonable people, I'd never seen anything like this. The fun quotient went down to zero, and some of my best people started to quit. We all recalled the famous cartoon of the old whaling ship's captain telling the crew, "The lashings will continue until morale improves." Why did I put up with this kind of treatment?

I didn't. I began to push back and got into several heated arguments with both Sharon and Gail. There were some ridiculous projects they asked for that I simply told my department not to do. When they harassed someone for not doing it, they were told I had canceled it, and they came after me. I'd tell them it was a useless, make-work project, and if they wanted to go argue its merit in front of Jennifer Blue, I was ready to go. I held an ace or two, as Jennifer had asked me to merge my company with theirs, and I was considering it. At that point they'd back off. After one of these confrontations Gail came up to me the next day and said she felt "violated" by my arguments. I said I was sorry she felt that way, but if she didn't like it she should stop "violating" the people in my department.

Then another person quit. I had known Ben for five years, and knew he was no wimp. He pushed back when the two "wicked witches," as they became known, tried to intimidate him. But he grew tired of being treated badly and went to another agency for the same money but better working conditions. And about this time I got the story on why Susan, the prior media director, had left. I realized that as long as the "wicked witches" from the East and West were allowed to treat people this way, I couldn't hope to build a department—good media professionals simply won't stand for that kind of treatment. I went to Jennifer and told her that. We both laid our cards on the table, with me telling her that Sharon and Gail treated people in an unacceptable manner, and it would be impossible to build a department unless it stopped. Whether it was due to all the money she was making, or another factor, she replied, "Well, these two are thoroughbreds, and you have to let thoroughbreds run at full speed."

I saw the light and dropped whatever thoughts I had had about joining up with Ferra/Blue. I was potentially giving up some money, especially if and when a conglomerate came in and bought Ferra/Blue, but the old Y&R expression came back: "It's a great place to work if your parents can afford to send you there." This was definitely not that type of place, and I knew it wouldn't change. I told Jennifer I'd help her find a permanent media director, but it wouldn't be me. We soon found them a permanent media director, a woman from a large Chicago agency, and we went our separate ways.

CHAPTER SIXTEEN

Avoiding "The Hitler Channel" at All Costs

We soon learned that when you're out on your own, in a small agency, you get approached by all kinds of wackos and weirdoes that would never get past the gates of a large agency. We got a taste of that shortly after we started when we got a call from someone representing the "Bagwan," the cult leader who was being deported from Oregon at the time. The caller identified himself as Oliver Smith and said the Bagwan had eighty-five Rolls-Royce cars that needed to be sold. He wanted us to suggest places to advertise these vehicles, but there was a "kicker"—each Rolls had a mountain, floral, or skyline scene painted on its sides. Oliver offered us a nice commission if we could plan and place the media to unload the cars. We suggested *The Wall St. Journal* as the place to advertise. "How much does a page cost?" asked Oliver. We gave him the rate—ninety-five thousand dollars—and he thanked us and hung up. About twenty minutes later Oliver called back. "How many times does the ad run for ninety-five thousand dollars?" he asked. He sounded surprised and disappointed when we told him that was the price for one page, one time. We never heard from him again, though we later saw in the news that all eighty-five cars had been sold at auction in Dallas.

Shortly after that we went to work for W.F. Young, makers of Absorbine Jr. It's a product that's over one hundred years old, that some people use for muscle pain relief and others use to cure athlete's foot. Despite its efficacy in both areas, only 15 percent of its purchasers use it for both ailments. It started out as a horse liniment, and grew from there, but was still marketed to horse owners in another form.

The company was located in Springfield, Massachusetts, and was owned by the Young family, whose many members depended on it to provide a very nice lifestyle. One day I got a call from Frank Von Wilfred, head of a local agency in Atlanta that specialized in healthcare products. He had made contact with the president of W.F. Young at a trade show, and had been invited to pitch the Absorbine Jr. account. "Who's their current agency?" I asked him. "J. Walter Thompson, New York," he replied, adding, "they've had it for twenty years."

I was skeptical about the possibility of a small Atlanta agency stealing an account from the giant JWT, but Frank told me the circumstances. Absorbine's media budget was less than two million dollars, a pittance to JWT's New York office, where twenty million dollars would get a client some attention. In fact, Frank told me, they fedexed Absorbine's annual plan to them in Springfield, not bothering to make a trip to present it in person. The creative abilities of Frank's agency combined with our media expertise could convince them to come with us, he believed.

We put together a campaign for Absorbine Jr. that used a few older celebrities as endorsers and planned the commercials to run on a variety of appropriate cable TV networks. A small group of us flew to Springfield, home of the Basketball Hall of Fame, and pitched the business. In addition to the formal pitch that afternoon, we were all invited to dinner with the Young family that evening. It was held at an elegant restaurant, and was a very pleasant affair. Besides the father-and-son team who ran the company, in attendance were sisters, brothers, aunts, uncles, and in-laws. The unstated but obvious purpose of the dinner was to check out the new agency for both their marketing savvy and personal savoir faire before handing over their advertising account. While conducted under luxurious conditions, it was as much a new business presentation as had taken place that afternoon in the offices of the W. F. Young Company. We passed, due in great part to Frank's ability to schmooze the upper classes; his house on Martha's Vineyard didn't hurt either. JWT made a token effort to defend the business, but a week later the decision was made in our favor.

Besides having a long-term relationship with Frank's agency, we learned a good lesson: there were accounts out there using big agencies, which were ignoring them; they made great targets for the expertise **and** the attention we could provide them. One client we picked up was Southeast Software, a hot company in Atlanta that was eventually bought by IBM. Southeast's chairman and founder was a dynamic man named Joseph Ansley, who had started his career as a salesman for Univac in the early days of computers. He insisted on meeting all new employees and everyone who did any work for Southeast, even though the company had grown to several hundred employees and over a billion dollars in sales.

We had several meetings with Mr. Ansley during the time we worked for Southeast and found him to be a savvy businessman as well as a great motivator who generated admiration and loyalty from his employees, at least most of them. He told us of an incident that had taken place a few months earlier in their offices. The executive committee was having a meeting, and the discussion turned to cutting expenses. The CFO suggested the company reduce the number of limousines it kept. Nobody was sure of the exact number on hand, so Mr. Ansley picked up the phone and called the company garage. "Southeast garage," a voice answered.

"How many limousines does the company have?" asked Mr. Ansley.

The voice responded again: "We have five for general use, and one more that we keep in reserve for Fatty, our chairman,"

Mr. Ansley was a little taken aback, but quickly responded by asking, "Do you know who this is?"

"No, I don't," said the voice.

Very firmly, Mr. Ansley stated, "This is Joseph Ansley, your chairman."

There was a pause at the other end of the line. Then the voice asked, "Well, do you know who **this** is?"

"No, I don't," responded Mr. Ansley.

"**Good**," said the voice at the other end, as the phone slammed down. Mr. Ansley laughed as he ended his story. He was one of our favorite clients, and when IBM bought his company our duties were taken over by IBM's agency. He sent us a nice letter of thanks for our work, which we later used in our efforts to get in the door of some high-tech companies as the dot-com era began.

Very early on in our struggle to get off the ground, we got involved in political advertising, as candidates poured more and more money into television. In 1986 an Atlanta attorney named Don Gaines jumped into the Democratic party primary race for the U.S. Senate. Don had little money, but traveled around the state in a van, using the "grass roots" method of campaigning. His idea was to generate local publicity in newspapers and radio, which he hoped would then lead to contributions for TV advertising. In case that didn't work, Don had an ace in the hole—his father-in-law was the chairman of American Airlines, and he was counting on him to loan or give him enough money to buy TV.

Unfortunately, Don was facing a strong Republican incumbent senator, Mack Mattingly. And then Wyche Fowler, who later won the Senate seat, jumped into the Democratic primary race. Don quickly became a long shot, raised very little TV money, and ultimately dropped out of the race—his father-in-law had decided not to put any money on the table.

But we had placed the little TV advertising that Don did, and we were hooked. All TV stations required political advertising to be paid upfront, which meant that we got paid upfront as well. The people in politics were always interesting, including their campaign staffs. And there was a firm end date to the campaign—election day—at which time you knew if you'd won or lost. Kim and I decided that we'd go after political advertising whenever we got the chance. And in order to keep our ethics and political preferences intact, we established the following commission structure:

Republicans	7.5%
Democrats	10%
Communists	15%

Don's campaign manager in 1986 had been a lawyer from Texas, Larry English. When Don withdrew from the race, Larry decided to move back to Dallas. He had just gone through a wrenching divorce and must have had a lousy attorney or been caught doing something naughty. He packed everything he owned—and I mean everything—into his car for the drive back to Dallas. Kim and I had breakfast with him on the day he left, watched him pull away from the IHOP, never expecting to see him again.

In 1990 another election cycle came around, and early one spring morning I took a call from a "Mr. X." An overly incredulous, mocking voice asked, "You guys are still in business?" "Yes, Larry," I responded, "and you're still alive?" Larry had returned to Atlanta to run a campaign for a candidate running for secretary of state, an elected office in Georgia. He told me what he was doing, and said he wanted K&M to place the television schedules for Tom Ready, an Atlanta attorney, unknown throughout the state. I immediately asked Larry how much money was in the war chest. "None," he replied, "we used all of it to produce our commercial." "Jesus Christ," I said, "how much did the commercial cost?" "Just under five hundred dollars," Larry responded. "I filmed it myself."

Sure enough, he had filmed Tom standing in a rough, deteriorating downtown area, speaking directly into the camera. To paraphrase Tom's message: "I'm Tom Ready, and I'm running for secretary of state. If you elect me, I'll lower the crime rate, no ifs, ands, or buts." They had hit on an area of concern to many people, and hammered that theme home. Money was raised on a daily basis, and Tom won the primary in July. After the primary, money came in a little faster, but we couldn't match what the incumbent secretary of state was spending. We bought TV time on a daily basis, as Tom's contributions came in. Larry moved his office into ours and worked constantly. When he started orchestrating "dirty tricks" on the phone, I'd leave the room to maintain "plausible deniability."

Tom Ready upset the incumbent and won a squeaker, but he won. With a few exceptions the Democrats won most of the statewide races that year. Tom became secretary of state and named Larry as his chief deputy. Crime did go down over the next few years.

About this time, Kim told me he and Liz wanted to return to Dallas. Having lived in Texas for six years, I know how much Texans love their state. If they ever leave, they always go back to Texas, and I understand why. Kim and I worked out an agreeable buyout, and he returned to Tracy-Locke. We stay in touch to this day, and get together whenever one of us visits the other's city.

In 1994 Tom ran for reelection as Secretary of State, and was expected to win handily. He had a sizable war chest and a good record on which to run. K&M was again hired to buy the TV time, and it looked as if it would be an easier campaign to win. But then the campaign made a mistake. Larry wouldn't be the campaign manager, as that would require him to take a leave of absence from his state job. Instead, they appointed a young, relatively inexperienced politico as campaign manager. And instead of making strong, inexpensive, right-to-the-point commercials, they got fancy. Money that could have been spent buying more TV time was put into making pretty commercials, and the campaign staff was enlarged with several high-paid "advisors."

Two other factors came into play as well. First, the Republicans nominated a smart young attorney to run against Tom. He ran a simple, hard-hitting campaign, similar to the one that Tom had run in 1990. Second, the Republicans surged nationally in the 1994 election, as they won a majority in the U.S. Congress and other races. All these factors lead to a surprising defeat for Tom. The state elected a Democratic governor, but several other Republicans also won key races in the state. Joe Ossendorf became the next secretary of state, and Tom returned to his law practice. He was the last Democrat for whom we worked.

In 1996 we hooked up with an old acquaintance from the

Republican party, whom we had done some work for earlier. Donald Solon was a savvy political advisor, and had worked against us in 1994, as he served as an advisor to Joe Ossendorf. The Republicans needed a candidate for a congressional race in an Atlanta district that was heavily Democratic. Donald agreed to run as the sacrificial lamb and hired us to place his media. Sure enough, he lost, but we gave it a good try, and he liked our style. We became friends.

Nineteen ninety-eight came around, with another election for secretary of state. We had stayed in close touch with Donald, and he got us an audience with Joe Ossendorf, who was running for reelection. I thought it was a long shot to go from working for one candidate in 1994, then his opponent in 1998, but wanted to give it a try. We talked with Joe, assured him we'd work hard for him, and with Donald's endorsement, won his approval. Joe now had the war chest of an incumbent, and he won reelection easily. In fact, he got more votes in Georgia that year than any other Republican candidate, including the multimillionaire who ran for governor and spent fifteen million dollars.

In a twist on what we normally did, I got a call one day from an attorney in Atlanta. Albert Goss was representing an enterprising tobacco farmer in North Carolina who had started his own cigarette company a few years prior. This isn't too unusual, as there are several small cigarette companies in tobacco country, just as there are lots of small wineries in California. Here was the unusual part: Mr. Brandy, the founder of Brandy cigarettes, had tried to place and sponsor a "Brandy" car on the Winston Cup racing circuit. I had to interrupt him as he explained the situation to me. "You mean he wanted to advertise another brand of cigarette on the **Winston** Cup circuit?" I asked.

"Correct," Albert responded and continued. Mr. Brandy had hired a driver and placed Brandy cigarette ads and logo on a racing car. After running in two races, the Brandy car had been banned from the track at the next race. The driver had been physically restrained from getting into his car, and prevented from participating in a race in South Carolina. In a civil action, Mr. Brandy was suing Winston's parent company, R.J. Reynolds

Tobacco, for restraint of trade. And for good measure he was also suing NASCAR for the same thing.

I told Albert that I wasn't a lawyer, but I didn't understand how someone could expect Winston to let a competing brand of cigarette to participate in a racing program that it supported financially and essentially owned. He told me not to worry about that aspect of it. All they wanted me to do was to serve as an expert witness and testify as to how valuable advertising can be to a racing audience, which statistics show contains a high concentration of heavy smokers. I'd need to do some preparation, and appear at a deposition, then testify at the trial, if it came to that. It sounded interesting, and I'd get paid to do it. I told Albert that with some research I could provide the estimated media value of racing audiences to a cigarette advertiser.

In preparation for the deposition I gathered all the available information I could find on auto racing, including its audiences and their characteristics. They were indeed heavy smokers, and obviously desirable to a cigarette marketer. Gee, maybe that's why Winston got involved in the first place, I thought. After a few weeks I had all my facts and figures organized, and sent them to Albert, along with my resume and other professional "credentials." Albert kept me informed about how the "discovery" stage of the trial was going. Mr. Brandy had been deposed, along with several other key players.

The day arrived for me to be deposed by the opposing attorneys, one from R.J. Reynolds and one from NASCAR. They flew into Atlanta and we convened in the conference room of a major law firm, along with several lawyers and a court reporter to transcribe everything. Albert said he would be sitting next to me at the conference table, and if he tapped my foot with his, I was to shut up or back off from what I was saying. I felt confident, as I had presented to many tough and skeptical clients before. Over the years I've been treated badly on occasion while presenting recommendations, and my recommendations have sometimes been rejected outright, with little diplomacy involved. But these two attorneys were something else.

I started to think I might be in for a rough time when one said, "Now, anytime you feel you need a break, or want a glass of water, just say so, and we'll stop." They worked me over, but good. They were always polite and professional, but disparaged everything I said, beginning with my background and experience. After questioning me about my overall experience, they zeroed in. "Have you ever worked on a cigarette account?" they asked. I admitted that I hadn't. I knew that would be a point in their favor as the deposition was read by a judge or anyone else. Then they started attacking the whole foundation of media decisions:

> Q: "How do you know how many people are watching a race on TV?"
> A: "We get ratings from the A. C. Nielsen Company."
> Q: "Nielsen? What's their sample size? How do they know exactly? Oh, so it's not exact? Then how do you know your estimated audiences are correct? So, your estimates could be higher or lower than the actual number of viewers, right? Well, if your audience numbers aren't exact, then your estimated values aren't correct, are they?"

You get the idea. A judge or someone else from outside the advertising industry who read the transcript would react very skeptically to how media decisions are made. It **is** based on estimates, as it's impossible to physically count all the people who watch a specific TV program or read a specific issue of a magazine. Trying to explain how the business works to someone who wants to understand it is hard enough; to justify it to people who are trying to muddle it is impossible. Again, everything they said was courteous, but they were scoring points on paper. On a few occasions Albert would object to a question, and legal arguments would be conducted "off the record." All I could do was answer honestly, and try to explain how we conducted business. I felt I was getting beaten up, but the time went quickly, and before I knew it, lunchtime hit, and someone suggested we break.

As soon as the transcriber stopped typing for the record, the two opposing attorneys became different animals, friendly and joking around. They asked Albert and me if we wanted to join them for lunch. Albert agreed, I was surprised. Then I realized, the old saying was true: "Nothin' personal, kid, it's just business." So we went to lunch, had a nice discussion about sports (not car racing), politics, and our kids. After an hour we returned to the conference room and resumed the battle. On the way to the restaurant I caught Albert alone, and asked him how I was doing. "You didn't feel me kick you, did you?" he answered. I started to feel better about things. The afternoon session was more of the same. We quit about five o'clock and I was drained. Albert and I said our goodbyes to the opposing attorneys and stopped off for a drink. He gave me a grade of "B." "Not an 'A,'" he said, "because you didn't convince them to come over to our side." A weak joke, I thought, but that was good enough for me. I knew I'd earned my money that day.

A few days later I got a copy of the transcript to check for accuracy before it was submitted to the court. Reading it again was depressing, in that 20/20 hindsight came into play, and I kept thinking of how much better my answers could have been. There were only a few minor words to correct, and I returned the document to the court reporter, as instructed. A few weeks later the case went to court, and Albert called to tell me the result—the judge had thrown it out prior to trial. Our side had thirty days in which to appeal, but Albert said it was highly unlikely that Mr. Brandy would do so, and he ultimately dropped the suit. It had been an interesting experience, and I was sorry we hadn't prevailed, but I couldn't help thinking that my initial reaction to the premise of a competitor crashing into the Winston Cup series had been correct. But I didn't rush out to earn my law degree at night.

In September of 1998 we got a call from Roger Murphy, the COO of a large agency in North Carolina, McKinney & Silver. M&S was a well-respected independent agency whose top network TV buyer had left. This happened just as their biggest client, Audi of America, had approved a big campaign for the fourth quarter.

Roger asked if we could get Audi onto several upscale cable networks with such short notice. I said yes, if they were willing to be flexible in terms of specific programs. It was late to be buying fourth quarter, and automotive advertising was one of the largest advertising categories in cable TV. This meant that much of the best programming would already be taken, often with exclusive deals that locked out other automotive advertisers. Roger understood the situation, and we reached an agreement for K&M to negotiate a big schedule for Audi's A8 luxury sedan.

This was a great assignment for me, as I'd never worked on an automotive account before, and I wanted to see what nuances there were in what had grown to be the largest advertising category in television. Plus, I owned an Audi 5000 at the time, and knew them to be good cars. M&S had heard of me due to the game I had invented in 1990, *Network Negotiator*. Turner Broadcasting had bought it from me and sent 2,500 of them to network buyers around the country. Apparently there were a few still floating around in 1998. They were calling us in to pinch-hit, but I didn't care. The budget was big, the product was great, and the client understood the marketplace and would be reasonable.

The Audi A8 was their top-of-the-line sedan, costing seventy thousand dollars plus. It had everything in it, including fans that would cool the passenger cabin automatically if it was parked in the sun. And it had an all-aluminum body, making it lighter, but stronger than most other cars. Once again, German engineering came to the forefront. As I got to know people from Audi, they would tell me that their cars were better engineered than either Mercedes or BMWs, but they just weren't as good at marketing as their cousins.

The A8 commercial was designed to point out the strength and safety of the aluminum body. It used walking crash dummies to illustrate the point, as Beethoven's "Ode to Joy" was played as background music. The action took place in a dimly-lit crash-test lab, with the dummies walking around stiffly, as if they were alive. It was definitely not the typical "car-on-road" commercial, with the beauty shots of the car going around curves as it rustled leaves along the side of the highway. That was by design—Audi insisted that M&S **never** produce "car-on-road" commercials that looked like all the others. Audi's budget was smaller than Mercedes, BMW and the leading Japanese imports. It was up against a huge pool of advertising "clutter" that would bury "me too" commercials.

With its high price, it was obvious that A8's target audience was upscale: people with one hundred thousand dollars plus incomes, highly educated, professionals, owners of businesses, etc. In addition to those **demographics**, Audi used **psychographics** to define its targets. Audi wanted to reach people who were contemplative about the luxury car they would buy. They wanted people who, once in a position to buy a luxury import, wouldn't automatically run to BMW or Mercedes. Audi believed their cars were superior in comfort and performance to their competitors, and just wanted a chance to prove it. As they defined it, they wanted people who didn't "follow the pack," and would give Audi the chance to win their business.

All that meant that we'd concentrate their commercials on cable networks that reached those people. Nielsen provides the audience estimates for the demographic part of the equation. Judgment and intuition provide the psychographic part. We placed ads on the usual suspects such as CNN, CNBC, MSNBC, the Golf Channel, and A&E. To that list we added specific programs on HGTV, ESPN, The Weather Channel, and others. The History Channel delivers an excellent audience for Audi, and we proposed placing a heavy schedule there. Susan Thompson was my primary contact at M&S. She was the top media executive on Audi at the agency, and was an accomplished media professional. As we discussed various networks, she warned me of a cardinal rule about Audi's television schedules: under no circumstances was Audi advertising to appear in programming that had anything to do with World War I or World War II. As The History Channel was sometimes referred to as "The Hitler Channel," because of programming it carried on those subjects, so we had to be very cautious whenever we placed ads on that network. The other German and Japanese imports maintained the same policy.

At first I thought this might be overly sensitive on Audi's part, but I quickly found their caution justified. Shortly after the A8 commercials began running in mid-October we got calls from a few of the networks. They were passing on complaints from a very few of their viewers who claimed the commercials offensive to them. Some objected to the use of Beethoven's "Ode to Joy" as the background music, claiming it was one of Hitler's favorite tunes and had been used in Nazi propaganda films. Others said that the crash dummies represented prisoners in Nazi death camps, and asked that the ad be taken off the air. Even though they seemed "overly imaginative," these complaints were always passed on to Audi's headquarters in Detroit. While aware of the complaints, Audi didn't change or pull the ad, but continued to be very cautious about where they appeared.

Susan and I worked well together. She was tough and outspoken, but left no guessing as to where you stood with her. We shared a lot of the same philosophies, and both of us wanted the best for Audi, so things went well. The campaign was executed to everyone's satisfaction, and Roger Murphy told me that he wanted to continue the relationship. That was music to my ears. I flew up to McKinney's office in Raleigh, met several other people and was given additional network buying assignments.

As time went on I realized that not all the media executives at M&S were as professional as Susan. There were some occasional rough spots, but we eventually accomplished our tasks. Depending on which account we were assigned, we'd work with different media planners, supervisors, or associate media directors. As at most agencies, there were a few swelled heads. On one occasion, a media representative from New York who called on the agency made a comment about one of their top media executives, known for his arrogance: "Somebody ought to remind him that he's a media supervisor in freakin' Raleigh, North Carolina." That said it all.

The dot-com craze came in 1999 and 2000, and both McKinney and K&M got their share of those clients, some good, some bad. In 1999 M&S was bought by a high-tech company that served dot-coms, so they got even more business from that segment. It was good business to have, as the networks required dot-coms to pay upfront, based on the early failures that were soon to spread around the dot-com world.

One high-tech company that we worked on was MegaOne. Its stock had soared, and it went on an acquisition binge, buying up other high-techs until it was fairly large and diversified. In early 2000 MegaOne had us explore the possibility of becoming a sponsor of the upcoming Olympics in Sydney. Because they were high tech, dealing with computers and the Internet, they competed with IBM in several areas, even though their sales were a fraction of IBM's. IBM was a major, longtime Olympic sponsor, guaranteed exclusivity from its competitors in many categories. In fact, they had negotiated a list of about twenty pages of exclusive protection, covering most of the areas in which MegaOne operated. It looked as if MegaOne was locked out of the Olympics.

But they didn't give up. Their commercials were very esoteric, in that they never mentioned the company's name (though it did show its logo at the end of each spot) or said what the company did. This was typical of a lot of dot-com advertising, which some gurus think contributed to their demise. MegaOne pressed us to push NBC to accept them as a sponsor. Their commercials were sent to NBC for review by their lawyers and top management. Upon seeing how nebulous the ads were, NBC said, "Let's give it a try." So MegaOne became an Olympics sponsor to the tune of about fifteen million dollars, which compared to an estimated fifty million dollars for IBM. The plan was to run MegaOne's ads and hope that IBM wouldn't object, either because they'd consider MegaOne too small to worry about or, because of the vague content of the commercials, wouldn't see them as a conflict.

In the interim, MegaOne could promote itself as an Olympic sponsor to its customers and employees, with all the prestige and status that came with the association. And there were other benefits. As part of the deal, sponsors got invited to Sydney as guests of NBC for a few days. Along with some MegaOne executives, NBC invited Karen and me along. We went, and when I say everything was first class, I mean it. It was the biggest and best boondoggle

I'd ever taken. We stayed on the *Seabourn Sun*, docked in Sydney's Darling Harbor, and went to the opening ceremonies, as well as several competitions.

One of the trip's highlights was meeting up with an Australian named Peter Guppy. Peter and I had lived on Sumatra as kids, while both our fathers worked for Caltex Petroleum. Our family had left Sumatra in 1960, and Peter and I hadn't been in contact for forty years. Prior to leaving the States, we tracked him down on the Internet from among Australia's nineteen million people, and called him. It turned out he was officiating at the Olympic tennis matches, and was in Sydney for the Games. Karen and I took Peter, his wife, and daughter to dinner at one of Sydney's many fine restaurants, where we did a lot of reminiscing. And in a bit of real irony, Peter was also in the advertising business—he sold space for a chain of Australian newspapers.

The day after the opening ceremonies we got the overnight ratings for the U.S. They were lower than NBC had estimated, but weren't terrible. They remained down, as the time difference and instant results from the Internet came into play. On the second day, IBM realized who MegaOne was and declared it a competitive advertiser, disallowed by their exclusivity agreement. They demanded that NBC pull MegaOne's schedule immediately. Did NBC comply? Is fifty million dollars bigger than fifteen million? They pulled us off so fast we hardly had time to inform the brass back at MegaOne's headquarters what had happened. Nobody was really surprised, but we had hoped we'd stay on the air a little longer. All of us stayed through our scheduled five-day rotation in Sydney, then flew home. MegaOne's unspent Olympic money was quickly reallocated to other NBC sports programming and some top-rated primetime shows later in September.

Late in 2000 we acquired another high-tech client in California. Zebo sold DSL lines to individuals and businesses at very low rates. So low, in fact, that they quickly went out of business. Their director of marketing was a twenty-six-year-old who said "dude" a lot, and it was the first and only time I've worked with a client who had a nose ring.

Just before they went under, they lured an older, more experienced man to be their marketing director. He arrived with a lot of stock options and a favorite agency in San Francisco. We were fired within two weeks of his arrival, and three months later Zebo declared bankruptcy and folded. All two hundred employees were put out of work. It was a fairly common occurrence, and made me think of all the careers and lives that the dot-com craze altered, and in many cases, ruined, while a few got rich. Several of my friends, many with kids, left the "bricks and mortar" companies for the glamour and promises of a dot-com, only to have their new company collapse around them. Some were able to get back to the relative safety of an established company, but some became consultants or took their depleted savings and bought a little business of some kind.

In 1999 we got the opportunity to work for International Paper. Their Consumer Paper Division in Memphis hired us to plan and place media for their HammerMill and Great White copy papers. I was amazed at how the copy paper business worked. It was a commodity business, with several companies trying to turn commodity products into true "brands." IP had instituted a classic brand manager system, bringing in a slew of very competent marketers from various package-good advertisers, including Coke, P&G and Gillette.

K&M planned and placed media for our initial two brands, as well as others that IP developed. The main objectives were to reach not only small business owners who bought their own paper, but also the managements of the big three office superstores—Office Depot, Office Max and Staples—where 80 percent of copy paper is sold to those business owners. Playing ball with those three chains is essential, as they control the copy paper distribution channels. Whenever we planned media, a key question was always, "How do we make sure that the key executives at the office superstores see it?"

By 2000 we had earned the media assignment for all the IP consumer paper brands, a wide variety of papers with many purposes. The HammerMill brand alone has over seventy types of paper, for example. Working again with Frank Lane's consultancy, we placed HammerMill commercials on upscale cable programming and into business magazines to reach owners and managers of small businesses. The copy appealed to those people, letting them know that HammerMill made papers for "everyday" use, and for those important occasions when people were presenting their best work to a client or customer. We put Jet Print Photo paper into pro and college football on network television, to reach people who wanted to save their digital photos on good paper. For Specially Yours, a paper for people who made their own greeting cards, we bought schedules in women's and craft magazines. Business for IP and K&M was good.

In the summer of 2000, Great White, known by many people as the "Shark Paper," celebrated the twenty-fifth anniversary of *Jaws* with a big network radio schedule. We also scheduled *Jaws* trivia contests and other local radio promotions tying in with the classic movie. Included in the four-hundred-network radio announcements we bought for Great White were eight spots on *The Dr. Laura Show*. This was right at the time when Dr. Laura was coming under fire for her comments on homosexuality. Various groups had called for a boycott of companies that advertised on either her radio or TV show. P&G, along with a few other major advertisers, had decided not to advertise with her, even though her radio show was rated second only to Rush Limbaugh's program at the time.

We bought just a few spots on Dr. Laura's show, thinking we'd be safe. Only two of the eight had run when we got the call nobody wants to receive. "What the hell are we doing on *Dr. Laura*?" asked IP's director of marketing. I explained our rationale for including her program on the schedule—large audience, heavily female, so as to balance out the higher number of men we'd be reaching with a lot of sports programming. He understood, but told us to get out of all the remaining spots on her show as soon as possible. Complaints about Dr. Laura had come not from the general public, but from a few secretaries within IP's headquarters. That made it even more urgent that we get out. We did so immediately, substituting other programs for her show.

IP's Marketing Department issued an E-mail to all employees, announcing that no more spots would run on Dr. Laura's show, and apologizing for the two that ran. The "incident" was an example of how sensitive advertisers have to be these days. Not only do they have to be careful not to offend current and potential customers, they have to be cognizant of all types of special-interest groups, as well as their own employees. Some creative gurus claim this is one reason why, in their opinion, there is so much ineffective advertising out there today—strong creative messages get watered down so they won't offend, they lose their punch, and the message doesn't register with its intended audience. In this case, all was forgiven, and we moved ahead with several successful campaigns. We continued to work for IP for several years through changes in their marketing personnel, philosophy and spending levels.

IP paid us directly, and I often held checks from them for several million dollars. At one point it struck me that something significant had happened. Years ago, while working at Waccabuc Country Club, I had waited on the president of International Paper, a member there. Now, thirty years later, I was again making money from the president of International Paper. Maybe it was the wine, but one night at dinner with some of the IP brand managers, I got the sense that things had come full circle. It was a good night.

EPILOGUE

As 2000 drew to a close, and the new millennium began, the advertising boom continued. It was driven by the strong economy, both high-tech companies and older sectors such as automotive. The dot-com craze continued as well. As more and more IPOs came about, advertising agencies and the media benefited from their spending. Many companies going public were mandated that as part of their IPO they would spend millions of dollars in advertising, designed to drive customers to their Web sites. Wall Street hadn't helped Madison Avenue so much since stock trading commissions were deregulated and the major brokerage firms began advertising to Main Street.

Orders and money began pouring into TV networks, radio stations, magazines, and other major media outlets, often coming in over the transom. One magazine ad director told me he ordered two extra fax machines just to handle all the extra (and often unsolicited) orders. Not surprisingly, he also told me that someone from the accounting department questioned the expenditure of eight hundred dollars to ensure that millions of dollars of orders were received promptly and accurately. The ad director won that battle.

For many media outlets the orders came in so fast that their sales reps didn't know what the company did, let alone who the players were at those companies. Magazines grew fat with new advertisers, cable networks sold their time at the top end of their rate cards, and radio stations charged the dot-coms premiums to bump other advertisers to get on the air.

The media quickly saw the money coming in from some companies that were little more than ideas, with many of them going bust in a short time. So almost all of them demanded cash upfront for dot-com companies, or forced their agencies to guarantee payment. Due to carelessness, arrogance, or gullibility, a lot of agencies got burned before they learned to collect their money upfront.

Then the good times rolled, as inexperienced people became marketing directors at many dot-coms. Often they just wanted outrageous, attention-grabbing ads, never mind the strategic thinking that should precede creative development and commercial production. Then they bought ads all over the place, including thirty-second spots in the Super Bowl for $1.8 million. For some companies, that $1.8 million was more than they had in sales! And when they advertised on the radio or in magazines, they'd often pay rate card prices, never negotiating down to prevailing rates. They didn't care. Their IPOs said they had to spend so much on advertising, but they didn't say they had to spend it wisely.

Then the dot-com bubble began to burst and the 9/11 attack occurred. Most advertisers stopped advertising, some for longer periods than others. It was like ten 747s had crashed all at once, with the resulting halt in airline advertising, except that it affected virtually every advertising category. And it lasted longer than any halt before. As weeks went by, hard-charging sales reps made calls on agencies and advertisers knowing that they wouldn't get an order, but just to keep relationships alive.

The 9/11 impact was so severe that annual advertising expenditures declined for the first time since World War II from 2000 to 2001. They were down 6.5 percent, according to *Advertising Age*, but started increasing in May of 2002. Robert Coen, McCann-Erickson's dean of the advertising expenditure trackers, estimates that ad spending rose 2.4 percent in 2002 and will increase by 4.6 percent in 2003. That puts spending back on track, but agencies, publishing and broadcasting companies have cut jobs over the last few years that they may not replace as business improves. That means more work for fewer people, with more and more people on the beach.

In fact, I currently know more **good** advertising pros, who are out of work than I've ever known at one time since I started in the business. A lot of folks are having their first experiences looking for jobs on the Internet. From everything I've been told, it's a little more efficient than looking the old-fashioned way, but not any more fun. And it doesn't necessarily speed up the process either. One senior marketing director I know went to his boss' office in mid-December of 2001. Since his division had made all its numbers for the year, he thought he was going to get a pat on the back, a bonus, and a nice raise. Instead he got whacked, along with some other senior people in the division, simply because the company needed to cut costs. It took him almost eighteen months to land a new job.

Despite the Internet's influence on job searches, at least two things have remained true: contacts count, and you still have to sell yourself face-to-face to close the deal on that great new job.

There are several good books out now about the various trends within the advertising industry—brand proliferation, media consolidation, creative techniques, etc. And there are books out that address trends that impact advertising, such as the rise of retailers' importance in the marketing process. There's even a book out that questions the efficacy and future effectiveness of advertising.

Whatever you choose to believe will happen to the advertising business, you can bet that it will continue to attract people who thrive on pressure, like working closely with other people, and understand human motives. They are gamblers, willing to forego the "security" of working for a big company. In return they get the adrenaline rush of solving problems and meeting tight deadlines. As a bonus, they're never bored, and they meet interesting people from all walks of life. One of advertising's icons, Jerry Della Femina, wrote a book that came out at about the time I first entered the business. In it, he described advertising as "the most fun you can have with your clothes on." He's right. And you're fighting wars at the same time you're having all that fun. It's paradoxical, but true, and I hope it always stays that way.

12/29/03